LISTEN TO MEN'S MOST PRIVATE
THOUGHTS ABOUT SEX...

"I figure if she fakes the second orgasm, it's not so bad. At least I'm sure she got some... ...ke such a jerk asking."

"When women placate... ...he expense of being their o... ...re also taking something a... ...they're taking away his challenge, making it too easy for him to get fat, lazy, and complacent."

"Women's assurances don't do much to ease men's fears and frustrations about size and erectile hardness. She can swear he's virile; and he won't believe her. He'll think she's being kind. His thinking is, if she loves him, what else would she say?"

"My second wife isn't always in the mood for sex. She can get every bit as hot as the first one did, but she has, thank God, her off days. You don't know how nice 'Not tonight, dear, I've got a headache' can sound sometimes."

...and much more!

WHAT MEN *Really* WANT

STRAIGHT TALK FROM MEN ABOUT SEX

(published in hardcover as
Dear Superlady of Sex)

SUSAN CRAIN BAKOS

ST. MARTIN'S PAPERBACKS

What Men Really Want was published in hardcover under the title *Dear Superlady of Sex: Men Talk About Their Hidden Desires, Secret Fears, and Number-One Sex Need.*

WHAT MEN REALLY WANT

Copyright © 1990 by Susan Crain Bakos.

Cover photograph by Kaz Chiba.

Library of Congress Catalog Card Number: 90-36884

ISBN: 0-312-92638-3

Printed in the United States of America

St. Martin's Press hardcover edition/October 1990
St. Martin's Paperbacks edition/December 1991

10 9 8 7 6 5 4 3

For Don Myrus, who named me Superlady, and
Jack Kaplan, who taught me the part I didn't know

ACKNOWLEDGMENTS

I am grateful to the following people for their contributions:

Nancy Love, my agent, and Toni Lopopolo, my editor, who helped shape the book.

Susan Windle-Posner, who edited the Superlady columns at *Penthouse Letters*.

Liz McKenna, who edited "What Do Women Want?" at *Forum*.

Jack Heidenry and Merry Clark, good friends and trusted career advisers.

Richard Bakos and Tamm Koerkenmeir, the best research assistants in the world.

C. J. Houtchens and the Magazine Feature Writing group of Washington Independent Writers for their moral support and exquisite sense of irony.

All the men who have written to me over the years at *Forum* and *Penthouse Letters*.

And, especially, the men who responded to my questionnaire.

CONTENTS

....

INTRODUCTION: DOES THIS COUPLE HAVE ANYTHING IN COMMON?

....

"The male and female brains are different structurally, and probably chemically, and that means that male and female behaviors are going to be different—overlapping, but different." —June Reinisch, psychobiologist and Director of the Kinsey Institute

Several years ago when I first started writing for the *Penthouse* magazines, I thought I knew about men and sex. I had come of age during the sexual revolution, and as a member of the first sexually informed generation, I believed in male and female sexual equality —equal meaning basically the same. The readers of the *Penthouse* magazines slowly began to educate me.

In 1985, under the pseudonym Carolyn Steele, Dear Superlady of Sex, I began writing an advice column for *Penthouse Letters*. The advice, meant to explain women sexually to men, was both sassy and personal and based on comments from experts and other women. Two years later, under my own name, I started another column, "What Do Women Want?" for *Penthouse Forum*. At *Forum*, I was also a contributing editor and writer of many fact-based articles on sex techniques and therapy. I learned a lot during my association with these magazines.

Most importantly, I learned to view the male sexual experience as it actually is, not as my romantic heart or political mind would like it to be. The sexual differences between men and women are rooted in biology, not ideology. But the Machismo Myth, on the other hand, is as much our myth as theirs.

Initially, many of the letters from male readers appalled me. Like Nancy Friday, who wrote in the preface to *Men in Love* that she often felt like washing her hands after reading the fantasies men wrote for her study, I mentally wrinkled my nose when presented with this side of men not often seen by the women they know and love. They wrote about breast fixations and foot fetishes, their desire to dominate, and, surprisingly more often, their desire to be dominated by a whip-wielding woman in high-heeled black boots. They wrote about fantasies of younger women or the ménage à trois, especially of female twins with identical sets of oversized breasts, of lesbian sex between women who would turn away from each other to embrace them. They wanted numerical answers to questions about penis size and how long intercourse should last, statistical data they seemed to require from sex as much as from football.

Their language was often blunt and graphic, words and phrases roughly hewn from linguistic stone. Gradually I grew accustomed to that language. No longer distracted by the words that once had seemed offensive, I began to hear their doubts and fears pounding like a musical backbeat to every question they asked.

They fear sexual failure, and particularly they fear disappointing women. I have come to believe men love women deeply and want to please us sexually even more than they want to be pleased themselves. But they are not exactly like us. We are equal—equal meaning different than, but equivalent in value to. We are not the same.

Alfred Kinsey had clearly and cleanly exposed the sexual differences between the sexes by the early Fifties. His work is still considered the ultimate statistical authority on sexual behavior. Yet we have allowed our social politics and romantic fantasies to blind us to the total picture his dispassionate numbers draw for us, if only we would connect the dots.

Before Kinsey published *Sexual Behavior in the Human Male* in

1948 and *Sexual Behavior in the Human Female* in 1953, people, including the medical authorities, generally assumed that man got more pleasure from sex than woman did—and that his capacity for sex increased throughout his twenties and thirties, dwindling in his forties or fifties, being reduced to a minimal level of activity with "the male climacteric," a state believed to be akin to menopause. One of Kinsey's most startling revelations was that males reach their sexual peak in adolescence, probably at sixteen or seventeen. Their decline is gradual, but evident with each decade, and Kinsey disputed the notion of the male climacteric altogether. Men, he found, continue to be sexually active well beyond the age that was considered the decent cutoff point for lusty endeavors.

Women, on the other hand, become more responsive as we move out of adolescence, into the twenties and thirties, where we peak. We remain close to peak well into middle age, when there is only gradual tapering off. Our potential for sexual pleasure is far greater than anyone had assumed.

Kinsey saw the implications of his findings on the traditional marriage of older man to slightly younger woman, a union delayed until past the male prime and tying two people who would never be in sexual sync. He thought marriage worked, when it did work, in spite of sex, not because of it. Many sociologists attribute the growing acceptability of premarital sex partly to his findings. Before Kinsey, no one assumed young men *needed* their release.

His work has a slight male bias, because he studied the male first, then compared the female to him. The two sexes were, he concluded, more alike than different. Men reported more extramarital liaisons, but Kinsey believed man's desire for multiple partners argued a psychological, not a physical, need for sexual variety. The one significant, unexpected, and startling difference between male and female response was the sexual aging pattern. Kinsey speculated that the cause might lie in a chemical difference between the male and female brains.

Kinsey also debunked the myth of the male penis as ultimate satisfier. For the first time, an expert said that penis size does *not* correspond to female pleasure. Some women might find psychological satisfaction in the act of penile thrusting—but it was clitoral stimulation that produced orgasm. A man didn't need a large penis to satisfy a woman. Shocking concept in 1953!

Famed clinicians and researchers Dr. William Masters and Virginia Johnson, in their own landmark works, *Human Sexual Response* (1966) and *Human Sexual Inadequacy* (1970), reinforced many of Kinsey's conclusions, particularly in regard to the sexual aging pattern and the clinical irrelevance of the penis to female orgasm.

Their work, however, has a definite female bias. They compare the male to the female, rather than the other way around, as Kinsey did. In *Human Sexual Response*, they devote three times the number of pages to woman than to man. Most tellingly, in *Human Sexual Inadequacy*, the subject is more often man's inadequacy than woman's. (While men are responsible for their own problems with PE —premature ejaculation—they are also blamed in some cases for female frigidity and for inorgasmia, which is often attributed to extreme male domination.) Masters and Johnson clearly document the case for female sexual superiority. Yet they strongly favor traditional marriage, treating the couple, "the sexual unit," rather than the individual.

If their value system had been different, they might have become advocates of pairing older women with younger men or of multiple relationships for women and men. Kinsey speculated that the sexual aging pattern might have led to the double standard. It was, perhaps, man's means of socially controlling a partner he could not hope to control sexually. Given a different social and political climate and different personal ideologies, Masters and Johnson could have helped champion a new double standard with the traditional positions switched.

Recognized as the founding parents of sex therapy, they instead developed a style of treatment that basically changes male sexual behavior to suit female sexual needs. Women are generally given the lead role in guided sex therapy. Assuming the superior position, the woman tells and shows her man how to do what she needs to have done. Masters and Johnson also developed the "squeeze" treatment, a method that enables the male to control his ejaculation in order to give the female a more lasting and satisfying sexual encounter. Hers is usually the hand that squeezes the tip of the penis, shutting down the orgasmic response until it's desired.

Masters and Johnson have contributed immeasurably to the sexual well-being of couples. Largely thanks to their pioneering research, the door to female sexual potential has been thrown wide open. Ironically, they have also helped turn sex into work—work that is more often performed by men for the benefit of women.

The sexual—self-help—guidebook publishing explosion they inspired is a female orgasm—oriented business. The buyers are predominantly women. Do they share their newfound information with husbands or lovers? In a loving or hostile fashion? Or do they keep it to themselves, using it to shore up their negative beliefs about men? With few exceptions—most notably *Ultimate Pleasures: The Secrets of Easily Orgasmic Women* by Marc and Judith Meshorer, which teaches women what *we* can do for ourselves—the books are sexual how-to guides written for women and about managing men as lovers. They are marketed in bookstores in the section labeled "Psychology and Self-Help," a category dominated since the mid-Eighties by books on relationships and what men do wrong in them (the *Men Who Can't Love* genre) or books on how to trap a man into marriage. Taken as a group, these collected works make a strong statement about the sorry state of communication between the sexes.

The focus of all these books is on changing him—and on what's wrong with him if he won't change. No one questions, and rightly so, that men should understand and respect female sexual biology, which dictates that we will need more time than they to become aroused. But we have overcorrected our thinking from the BC (Before Clitoris) period dominated by Freud, who declared the only mature female sexual response was the vaginal orgasm produced by intercourse. Now we seem to be saying the only mature male responses, sexual and emotional, are those that correspond to *our* responses and meet *our* needs.

In their May 1989 special issue on sex, *Ms.* magazine said, "When male sexuality was the only model of sexual freedom, women tried out high-sensation, low-emotion sex. Now, women know that they want a man to 'make love like a woman.' "

The phrasing is interesting: not *to* a woman as she needs to be made love to, but *like* a woman. Where is the same respect and understanding of their sexuality that we expect men to grant us?

Let me remind you again of Kinsey's major discovery: the sexual aging pattern. This could be the single most important aspect of male psychobiology in the coming decade. The trend-setting baby boomers have plunged over the crest of forty. The women are at the height of their sexual powers; the men, declining. Will this man who is no longer driven by intense sexual need be willing to work so hard at sex in order to please us?

Yes, I believe he will, because his desire to please us goes beyond his need for release. He wants more to please us sexually than to be pleased himself. The average man does not want a woman lying still beneath him, a compliant vessel waiting to be filled. Women who believe that "All he wants is his own orgasm" are wrong. He wants more than anything to give a woman satisfaction in his bed. But whether we are the women he wants to satisfy certainly will depend on how we treat him, sexually and otherwise.

Women's sexual freedom has confused him. It's confused us, too. Ambivalence is a unisex condition. Yet he is the one blamed for everyone's conflicts and doubts. The truth is that women have vacillated between wanting the freedom to have sex without love and wanting sex to lead to commitment—just as we have vacillated between wanting equal rights in the workplace and also wanting the right not to work, to be supported by some man.

The sexual backlash has left women feeling embarrassed about our own sexuality again, but we can't fairly blame the renewed sense of repression we felt in the late Eighties on men. That backlash originated with the religious right and the extreme feminist left, two diverse groups with little in common except disdain for the bluntness of male sexuality and thinly disguised fear of the limitless potential of female sexuality. It was nourished by the media in stories about the aftermath of the sexual revolution, stories that capitalized on the growing dissatisfactions of single career women and the public's fear of disease.

Feminist groups have chosen to focus exclusively on the negative consequences of sex: unwanted pregnancy and abortion, rape, incest, sexual harassment and abuse. They treat every man as a potential rapist. The antiporn activists crusade against male sexuality, against the visual imagery often necessary or desirable to their arousal, seldom to women's. But the far more subtle antisex attacks are those by mainstream media, which are really attacks on women's sex lives—because it was *women's* sexual behavior, not men's, that had changed during the sexual revolution.

In *Re-making Love: The Feminization of Sex*, Barbara Ehrenreich, Elizabeth Hess, and Gloria Jacobs draw attention to "the little-discussed fact that the true heart of the sexual revolution was a change in women's behavior, not men's. 'There hasn't been a change in male sexual patterns in the twentieth century,' historian Vern Bullough told *Time* in 1984. As that article pointed out, 'Studies tend to agree that changes in male premarital sexual behavior since the 60s have been rather modest. Premarital sex rates for women more than doubled between the 60s and 1971, and sharply rose to a new peak in 1976.' "

Women are also almost as likely as men to indulge in premarital and extramarital affairs today. Even as they were reporting the latest sex-poll results, our magazines were telling us that men had conned us into "casual sex," which hadn't worked for us. In typical American fashion the editorial viewpoint was urging us away from an extreme of promiscuity few had lived anyway—the recent Kinsey report on sex and morality in the United States makes that clear—to a conservative, *prissy* point a giant pendulum swing away, where sex was used as Mother intended, as a reward, a weapon, an inducement to commitment. Instead of dealing with the confusion sexual freedom has produced in women, we choose to blame men for leading us into casual sex, for using us, then not wanting us when we decided the time for marrying and reproducing had finally come.

We measure him sexually by how well he matches our ever-changing criteria, determined only in part by what we really want and need in bed. He's a good lover if we have multiple orgasms . . . he calls back after the first time in bed . . . he wants to marry us. He, on the other hand, measures himself sexually by our physical responses to his lovemaking. A man *needs* to please a woman.

In recent years, we have sometimes treated men as sex objects or, more often, as success objects, bitterly castigating them when they fail to meet our sexual expectations, critically evaluating their suitability as mates based on their incomes and social status. We have tried to make them more like us in matters of love and sex—while at the same time wanting them to remain more like their fathers in their role as *provider*.

We have been excessively hard on them. Some time ago I began to suspect that the empress who tells us what to think about men and sex was wearing no clothes. Differences between the sexes do not exist, the empress says, except those differences that are flaws in the way men love women. And we can retrain him. He is she with a fatter paycheck.

No, he is not. I have studied the research data, and I have been privy to his sexual secrets, fantasies, fears, and longings. He is primarily an erotic visualist. His sexual language and imagery is more graphic than our own. His biology puts him at odds with ours, which gives us greater potential for sexual pleasure just as his potency is waning. While his innate need is to perform, ours is to attract. His orgasm is more certain, but our capacity for orgasm surpasses his.

Yes, men are different from us—but not less, not greater than, merely different. For some reason, this obvious conclusion is fought most vociferously by some women. Several angry women told me I'd reached my conclusions on men and sex based on the mail at *Penthouse*—and *Penthouse* readers are "the degenerate minority." So I developed a questionnaire and eventually distributed it to hundreds of men contacted through ads in upscale city magazines and other sources, including distribution by volunteers: friends, business associates, sex therapists, and medical professionals. Over a thousand men responded, many writing long letters sharing their thoughts and experiences, fears and fantasies. In addition, I interviewed more than a hundred men in depth. What they told me only reinforced the conclusions I'd reached.

I suspect men may even love us better than we love them. Certainly I love men better than I did before I knew them so well. Loving them doesn't mean being submissive to their power or blind to their faults—or loving oneself or women any less. It doesn't mean letting them get away with anything either! Love does mean acceptance, differences and all.

If any woman can have orgasms—multiple orgasms, extended orgasms, extragenital orgasms—a man can't *always* perform on demand, according to the standards imposed by our myths and his.

Sex is more dependent on male arousal than female. That is the crucial difference. They know it better than we do.

Part One

THE LANGUAGES OF LUST

Whose Voice Would You Rather Hear on Morning TV?

···

"I spent three days at home in bed with the flu. I heard all the talk shows, TV and radio. Mostly, they talk about sex. I never knew sex could be so boring. How do these pleasingly plump ladies in the audience summon up their tittering outrage?"

—A man

We certainly talk enough about sex. Every member of a "Donahue" audience can tell you that the first step toward solving any sexual problem is "communication." And she can spout the acceptable jargon. Sex has become a priority subheading in that vast self-help industry run by problem-solving professionals dedicated to helping us "work on" ourselves and our relationships. It is their voice we trust when the subject is sex.

Americans understand "erotic" the way the French understand humor. The French consider Jerry Lewis a comic genius; they don't "get" humor. We regard those brushed-to-perfection centerfolds as the personification of sexiness and/or sinfulness; we don't "get" erotic. The French intuit the erotic connection between men and women long before the age of consent, and not fearing it, fluently speak its language in verbal and nonverbal forms. *They* don't need a team of therapists to tell them if their orgasms are coming from the proper place or not. *We* believe ourselves fearless when we can speak clinically. We label the subject "sex," and focus obsessively on the mechanics, particularly the mechanical failures.

Our language of lust is really three languages: nongender speak, womanspeak, and manspeak. Here is a description of female orgasm in each language:

3

Nongender: "The subjective experience may differ, but the physiological cycle a woman goes through as she builds sexual tension, reaches orgasm, and returns to the initial resting place is the same for all women. This process [is] called the sexual response cycle. . . ." (From *For Yourself: The Fulfillment of Female Sexuality* by Lonnie Barbach.)

Womanspeak: "I know it's coming on when I'm overcome by a feeling of weakness. It's a total surrender, a giving up of yourself to the man you love, to love itself. It's an emotional release as much as physical. I feel it throughout my whole body when I'm really in love." (According to a thirty-year-old woman.)

Manspeak: "I shot my load up into her and felt her pour over my dick as she came." (From a letter sent to *Penthouse Forum*.)

Nongender speak is, of course, the choice of therapists, authors of sexual self-help books, talk-show hosts, and reputable journalists. The great noninvolved have given us words and phrases like "preorgasmic," "postcoital," "premature ejaculation," and "sexual response cycle," words meant to demystify sex by putting it on a level with cycles of a washing machine. The leading linguists are experts like Masters and Johnson, people who convey authority in this area as much by their lack of sexual allure as by their advanced degrees. Think of sex as a subject covered by the daily thirty-minute national news report, and you will recognize immediately that nongender speak is the controlled, yet urgent, voice of the news. After listening to it, you may not be able to locate Costa Brava or your G-spot, but you will be lulled into believing that you know now more than you did before.

The sex advice columns in women's magazines and everything under the imprimatur of an advanced degree are written in nongender speak. It is an absolute language in the area of mechanics, even though two experts speaking in the same tongue reach different conclusions. (There is or is not a G-spot. There is or is not a difference in clitoral and vaginal orgasms.) In the area of feelings, this language *makes no judgments*. Talk shows feature the linguists regularly.

Womanspeak is almost as politically correct as nongender speak. A reassuring murmur, it is a variation on the litany of daisy-petal plucking: he loves me, he is incapable of love, he loves me, etc. This language is largely spoken woman to woman in private, and by therapists, talk-show hosts, and some enlightened male authors in public. Womanspeak attempts less to demystify sex than to remystify it according to the currently acceptable standards for romanticizing sex. It deals in such matters as the number of orgasms deemed appropriate, from where they should emanate, and the conditions for surrendering your body to men—i.e., degrees of acceptable love. It has sentimental excesses not generally found in nongender speak—which may praise commitment, but not to the point of nauseating the uncommitted.

Off the air and outside the pages of women's magazines, womanspeak is spoken by all classes of women, who constantly address the quintessential female question: Will he call? Pink collars and business suits assure each other that yes, he *will* call again after you foolishly did it too soon, and no, nobody does it anymore except for love. Even if they're only twenty and single, they sound as if they've spent twenty years reading articles on putting the zing back into married sex. Womanspeak purports to tell the secrets: how to get him, keep him, win him back, explain it when he's gone.

Manspeak is spoken to men by men—and by those few female writers and editors at sex magazines who've learned the language from necessity, the way the expatriate American finally puts down his phrasebook and signs up for real lessons in a foreign language. In manspeak—a bleak and graphic language with its roots in the toilet talk spoken by grade-school boys—sex is reduced to its lowest common physical denominator: virtually indistinguishable variations on inserting tab A into opening B. ("I'd like to shove my (a) dick, (b) cock, (c) rod, (d) jackhammer into her (a) cunt, (b) pussy, (c) hole, (d) gash.") In womanspeak, sex is equated with the L-word. Manspeak brandishes the F-word—and can do so in menacing fashion.

Manspeak is usually spoken in places where women are not: within groups of men or written on pages sandwiched between photos of nude women. It is not meant to explain or demystify sex. Manspeak is penis talk, and the penis only knows up from down. It is the voice of bravado, the black humor of the soldier who tosses out expletives in the hope that "him" rather than "me" will be consumed by the opposing side. This is something women seldom understand. Manspeak is penile cheerleading.

Men in general understand the basic difference between the sexes and sex better than women do. They know the onus to perform is on them, which is *the* critical difference. Egalitarian or not, sex, as our society defines it, is more dependent on an erect penis than a naturally lubricated vagina. We have KY Jelly. They live with the fear of failure, and the sense of its inevitability, as we live with the fear of sexual desertion by them and the knowledge that sagging breasts are somehow more devastating than balding heads.

Recently, I was lunching with a male friend. We watched two attractive women walk past a table of men in business suits who were keeping one eye on the street and the passing parade. Their talk was punctuated by explicit comments about body parts. Manspeak. "Ballplayers," my friend said, relishing his double entendre. "Chatter in the field. If you're going to play the game, you have to talk it up all the time." The women, catching a phrase or two, wrinkled their noses.

They, of course, had been telling each other to send him cute cards because he hadn't called back.

1 | Womanspeak—As It Sounds in His Ear

••

"Women should be more straightforward from the start. Men are more direct. They don't like to play games about whether or not a woman is interested in sex. She comes on like she is, then says she isn't. But maybe she is anyway. Why can't she be clear?"

—An executive in his forties, earning over $75,000 a year

When the subject *isn't* sex, the subtext often is. People in the initial attraction phase lace their prosaic conversation with sexual innuendos, deliberately or not. Men tend to read sexual overtones into everything from a short skirt and black panty hose to a friendly smile. Conversely, when the subject *is* sex, the subtext sometimes isn't. While men think we're signaling erotic intentions in an outfit we copied straight from *Vogue* in an effort to impress other women, they complain that we want something else when we say we want them sexually. How do they get the idea we do if we don't? Or that we want more than sex—for instance, commitment or a baby—when we say we want only him?

There are two levels of talking about sex: I Want It, and Here's How I Want It. More confusion surrounds the first level, while the potential for real pain is greater at the second. Both confusion and pain are effective communication blockers. Even if you say what you mean clearly, men may not hear it. But the main factors influencing how men hear (or don't hear) what women say about sex on level one are the macho code and female dissembling.

Men who are living by the code may regard what we say as so much underbrush to clear in their mindless pursuit of machismo goals, which lay more emphasis on the motto "Be Prepared" than does the Boy Scout handbook. Writing in *The Intimate Male*, therapists Linda Levine and Lonnie Barbach identified the sexual requirements of "machismo," the Spanish term meaning maleness, dominance, courage, virility, and aggressiveness as:

Always are ready to have sex.
Always have rock-hard erections.
Always have unending staying power.
Always satisfy their women.

The key word is "always," and it weighs heavily upon men who, though they realize the standards are impossible, try to live up to them anyway. Machismo affects a man's hearing. You say no or maybe, and he hears yes.

The code also sets the sexes up as adversaries. He is determined to pursue, we to defend from his attack. He must hold back his own pleasure until we have had ours; we must be sure we get as much from him as we can before he does let go. We all agree this is a ridiculous state of affairs. Yet he is driven to persist; and he is not alone in his single-mindedness.

Adversaries naturally don't trust each other with the truth. They bury it beneath layers of manipulative lies. We say, "I don't want sex until I know you better," when we mean, "I want to be sure I've waited long enough to give in, so you'll call back." The "machisma code" says: *Men are always ready unless there is something wrong with them. Or us. An attractive woman gets her man—and, by the use of sex, gets her needs met through him.*

No, we don't always mean what we say or say what we mean. This is what men tell me they hear when we're talking about sex: dishonesty; manipulation; nonerotic need; disdain or distrust or dislike; and good feelings, including affection, desire, and love. Sometimes their assumptions are based entirely on the tone, not the content, of what was said. One man told me, "I completely changed my mind about what I thought a woman was saying to me when she began gently stroking my hair."

The most frequently asked question about sexual communicating is:

Why do women say they don't have sex on the first date—when they obviously do?

"I am forty, divorced, and been around. Recently I met an attractive blond woman in her late thirties at a classy neighborhood bar. After assuring me she never goes to bars and never gives her phone number to men she meets (in those bars she never enters), she gave me her phone number. I called her. Five minutes into the first date she told me she doesn't have sex on the first date. Several hours later she was passionately returning my kisses. She put her hand on the part of my trousers covering my stiff cock and squeezed until I was gasping for breath. When she unzipped me, I took it as a signal she meant to do what she said she doesn't do. The woman was a terrific fuck. I'm not complaining. But why do women still say no when they mean yes?"

I can guess what the attractive blonde meant him to think: She doesn't have sex with *any* man she's just met, and he was special. Probably he was. It does happen outside novels and films occasionally. Most of us can recall one time, can't we? Distrusting her sudden capitulation, he doesn't, however, believe this experience with him was her one time.

"I had a great affair with a woman who went to bed with me on our first date," says Eric, thirty-five and single. "She didn't tell me until months later she'd never done that with anyone before; and I believe her. I probably wouldn't have believed her if she'd told me then. But it was obvious from the start that we had a strong, very special attraction. I'm glad neither one of us messed it up by saying something which could have been taken as a lie."

Men still react with surprise, indignation, shock, or dismay when a woman does exactly what she says she doesn't do. The double standard is weakened, but not vanquished. Indoctrinated in the macho code of pursuit, they push ahead, expecting her to delay the seduction—even as they're pushing for it—until the need for it has become deliciously intolerable, which rarely occurs on a first encounter. (No, it isn't fair. We are talking about reality, not fairness.)

If they don't buy being her only "first," they also disbelieve they qualify for those other rare occurrences: the best, and the biggest.

"If a woman tells me I'm the best lover she's ever had, I know she's lying," says a forty-year-old chauffeur from the Midwest. "Maybe when you've been together awhile and you're really in love, you can say that in a believable fashion. It's not any truer, it's just believable that she would feel like that. Otherwise, I feel like a woman who lays on the lavish compliments about my skill in the sack says the same thing to every guy. She's probably been around more than I have. Flattery is part of her shtick."

A Pittsburgh computer analyst disagrees: "Sometimes two people really connect immediately. It's emotional and physical chemistry; and it is the best. Men should realize women say you're the best because they're very emotionally moved and they're speaking from the heart."

But the penis-size lie is the one they won't forgive.

From a divorced architect in his forties: "I was totally turned off by a woman who said, 'Oh, he's so big! He won't bite me if I touch him, will he?' First, I'm not big, only average. Why did she have to lie and spoil the mood? Second, she reminded me of my ex-wife, who had this nauseating habit of asking 'Can Petey come out and play?' when she wanted sex."

The second most asked communication question is:

Was she lying about what she wanted from me?

"A woman I've known as a casual friend recently propositioned me. She called me at work and said, 'I propose we go to bed together, no involvement, just sex.' Before she asked, I wasn't sure if I wanted to sleep with this woman or not, but what kind of man turns down such a proposition? It was my first; and in this day and age of sexual paranoia, it might be my last. In bed she came on super-aggressive—like a hard-boiled detective-fiction heroine doing a seductress shtick. It put me off a bit, but I recovered: nicely, I thought. She had several orgasms. Now she says she isn't interested in another go-around, because the sex wasn't so hot. Could you please explain? Did she want romance after all?"

It's always possible this man wasn't a four-star lover, since his heart wasn't in it. Perhaps rather than saying "You were lousy," his seductress spared his feelings and cut her losses. Or perhaps she was secretly hoping the staged sex would excite a romantic spark in both of them, because she wanted to want him. The dishonesty was maybe hers and surely his.

He should have said no or maybe, not yes, because he wasn't that interested in sex with her. Men unfortunately can't say *no*. They believe they can't refuse the request of any reasonably attractive female for their bodies any more than they could refuse fried chicken from a country grandmother. Whether they desire sex or not, they believe they should perform on command, or request. Then, if the experience isn't wonderful, they begin to suspect her motives.

Being in bed with a man who can't say no isn't like being in bed with a man who enthusiastically says yes. Don't call him first, unless you know he hasn't called for a very good reason, like you're his boss or married to his brother. An available man will approach an available woman when his desire is high enough. You can't count on him to say no.

A professor in his forties expressed a different opinion about the woman who boldly instigates a liaison, then doesn't want another: "Some women believe conquest is important. It's a reverse love-'em-and-leave-'em scenario. Some things take time to evolve, especially feelings and commitment. Often too much, too fast causes immediate burnout. I've run into more than a few women who aren't willing to put the time into it. They think the sex should be immediately fantastic—or they move on. Men aren't the only ones who do this."

Men are the ones who ask:

Why do women still use the granting of sexual favors to get what they want from men?

"I had dinner with an old friend the other night," said Juan, thirty-nine, who has been divorced for three years following a fifteen-year marriage. *"He asked me how I was doing after the divorce. I told him the women I meet all want something from me. They're types. The Queen Bitch wants to drain you of all your manly fluids; and that's all she wants. The Prospective Wife wants your name, sperm, and income, before she's too old to have kids. And the Cheating Wife is basically happy with the sex at*

home, but she's looking to trade up. If you make more money than her husband does, she wants you. My friend nodded his head in agreement. He didn't give me any argument."

I gave Juan an argument. Do you think I let him get away with dumping women into three broad categories? I demanded examples. He had them.

"I knew Suzanne was a Queen Bitch on the first date," he said. "She's bright and fun—I never had so much fun with a woman in my life—but she works at being tough. We had sex that first night. She was warm and responsive, but afterward she withdrew. The next morning she gave me the bum's rush out of her apartment. She hurt my feelings. I wanted to make love to her again that morning, but she was cold, rejecting. A few days later she called me. She was very warm and sweet again, because she was horny. Maybe you think men never feel sexually used, but we do. In one way it's flattering to know you can please a sexually demanding woman; in another way, it's dehumanizing."

There were the single women who told him they wouldn't have sex until they felt sure the relationship was going somewhere—and by somewhere, they meant the marriage track. And the ardent neo-feminists who demanded equal rights in the workplace, preferential treatment when the dinner check was presented, and multiple orgasms in bed. And the wives looking to upgrade to a more successful husband. "The last married lady was angry because her husband had never given her the house he promised her. The sex was fine with him, but she wanted that house. She said she would leave him for me after I told her I was buying a house. She said she would do things for me in bed no woman had ever done before."

Juan's story may be an extreme, but men who are married or otherwise committed frequently complain that a woman's granting of sexual favors is tied to a man's bestowing of nonsexual favors. (And many men believe spending money is their most erotic quality.) Women, too, say they trade favor for favor, cunnilingus for fellatio, extended afterplay for favored positions or being allowed to come in her mouth or on her body. Men, however, wrote about partners who were offering sexual favors in exchange for material goods or services rendered outside the bedroom. One man gave his wife a diamond bracelet for Christmas, and she responded by giving him this note: "XXX Entitles bearer to 52 blow jobs this year. XXX"

"When a woman uses sex to get you to behave in a certain way, she's manipulating you," says Matt, thirty-seven. "You can hear it in her voice when she asks if you'd like her to take your balls in her mouth—and you know she hates to have your balls in her mouth. It's going to cost you something. What I've learned to trust in a woman is *sexual* need. Give me a woman who wants to be fucked as badly as I do, who'll tell me how she wants it—and I'll be glad to give it to her. I'll give her more than I'm getting, as long as the giving is sexual."

"Women too often use sex as something they are holding for ransom," wrote an entrepreneur from the northeast. "They only reinforce all the bad old stereotypes when they behave like that. It gives them the ultimate control position—and if you want my opinion, women aren't ready to surrender that control. They are still the ones who decide if there will or won't be sex, and how it will be and when and where. If things were equal between lovers, they wouldn't have all the control, would they?"

Not all men shrink from emotionally or financially needy women. In fact, some men feel more potent if they believe a woman is, or is longing to be, dependent on them. Even these men, however, would like to feel the sex is independent of this other need.

"You can hear it in a woman's voice when she has to have a man to complete her life," says Jon, twenty-nine. "She might be spouting an independent line, but her voice will quake somewhere and give her away. She doesn't consciously use sex to wheedle little things out of you. Rather, sex is the theater where she plays the roles she thinks will win a man. She's read all the books and holds back until the third date, won't take your cock in her mouth until date four or five, and so on. She starts trying to win you from the first time she lets her hand rest lightly on your arm. Nothing impulsive about her!"

And according to Arthur, forty-nine, "I am beginning to meet women in their late forties who are looking for a pension plan. When they say they love sex but want to save it for something special, they mean for the day you put their name as beneficiary on your insurance policy. Can you imagine sex with a woman who thinks it's her means to a golden age? She's reassuring you about potential impotence—which she probably hopes to God you'll experience while you're still in your shorts."

Bob, thirty-four, who says he has begun to think of his dates as "ticking biological clocks with openings for my cock between the numbers," says, "I understand that women have deep needs and wants which have nothing to do with sex. So do men. What I don't understand is why they still try to get all their needs met through men—and why they can't disassociate wanting marriage or a baby or a better income from sex. When I want to fuck a woman, I forget all about my job dissatisfactions. She doesn't always forget hers. Maybe in the back of her mind, she's playing this tape, 'If the sex is good, he'll marry me; and I can quit my job and stay home with the baby we can make.' "

And some men ask:

Why do certain women put a man down even as they're coming on to him?

"Is it me she dislikes, or men in general, or what? I am thirty, and a lot of the women I date, who range from nineteen to thirty-five, have begun our relationship by sparring with me. They tease, taunt, and put me down constantly. I look down and their nipples are hard. Usually these gals are dynamite in the sack. Often they are surprisingly gentle and tender lovers, too. Why must everything they say have a cynical, aggressive edge to it? Why can't they just flirt? Men are accused of not saying what we mean, but women are worse at communicating than we are sometimes."

We live in cynical times, love. She probably thinks she *is* flirting. Maybe she reached flirting age when it was no longer politically correct to flirt. Then the practice became acceptable again. Where did she learn her technique? From reading "Cathy" comic strips and watching old "David Letterman" reruns on those rare nights when she didn't have to be at the office early the next morning. Be patient with her.

Here are the top ten reasons women attempt to repel even as they are trying to attract:

10. She would rather fantasize/masturbate than do it with a real man—unless she is sure he won't disappoint.
 9. She uses aggressive verbal pyrotechnics as a form of stress testing of prospective lovers.
 8. She really doesn't want sex until her thighs are thinner.
 7. She believes all that media hype about the death of sex.
 6. She's so comfortable complaining about the lack of good men to her women friends that she doesn't want to risk losing her spot in the whining circle by finding out you're good.
 5. She's really too shy to talk about sex, so she gives you the verbal equivalent of a punch in the arm instead.
 4. She has no condoms on hand and hopes to put you off until she can lay in a stash.
 3. She's hoping to intimidate you enough that you will not argue about her being on top.
 2. She is afraid of her own intense passion, which you have aroused.

And the number-one reason some women verbally repel the very men they want to attract: She doesn't want to fall in love any more than you do. Maybe she believed you when you gave her that line about looking for commitment.

Men, too, behave in rejecting ways—but seldom when they're attempting to seduce a woman. Even the most critical, put-down artist plays it soft when he wants to make love. Women who say brutal things while projecting desire probably do so to cover real feelings they aren't sure how to handle—or to push a man away when they don't know how to say no. But they perplex, confuse, and sometimes hurt men anyway.

"I don't expect a woman to say, 'Hey, let's fuck,'" says James, thirty-seven, "but I do think she could drop some verbal clues. I worked for six months beside a beautiful woman who kept telling me I wasn't her type and describing her other lovers to me in a very hard-edged way. After she was transferred to another city, one of her friends told me she'd really wanted me. Christ, I wanted her but I was afraid to show it.

"She was the sort of woman you're afraid to show your dick. You're sure she'd laugh."

Sometimes communication really does work. Men do say:

When my woman talks about sex with me, her eyes get soft. *"She's a little too shy to grab my penis. When she wants sex, she curls up next to me on the couch and strokes my arm until the hairs stand up. In bed, she'll tell me what she wants. I love the way she says things in that sweet, sexy whisper. When she says. 'Please lick around my clit,' I go nuts to please her,"* writes a Michigan hardware-store owner.

Some of the happy mail at *Penthouse Forum* details real or fantasized sexual experiences. Much of it, in praising a woman's loving ways, contains clues to what makes men hear an undercurrent of whispered love or affection, respect or regard, desire or passion beneath the most prosaic sex talk. Often they say she is good at asking for what she wants sexually without making them feel ignorant for not automatically knowing. They can hear a simple "I want you" a lot of different ways, depending on the tone of voice, body language, and the look in a woman's eye when she delivers the line.

"I respond more to the tone of a woman's voice when the mood is sexual than to what she's actually saying," says Alex, thirty-two. "If her voice is right, she can guide me; and I hardly know I'm being led. You can't hide true lust. It ripples through a voice beautifully."

"I like it when a woman tells me exactly what she wants," says Keith, thirty-four. "It's exciting to hear her say, 'Please stroke my clit' or 'Lick the skin inside my thighs, lick into my pussy.' That kind of instruction would only turn me off if she said it in a patronizing tone of voice, like, 'Boy, are you a dumb fuck for not knowing this.' Otherwise, I feel she really wants me; and she's helping me get to her by giving me directions."

There's nothing more flattering to a man than to believe he is the object of your truest lust. I don't think lust can be faked, any

more than you can "play" hard to get. Why should anyone, male
or female, want to fake it?

All You Need to Know About Sex Talk

- Don't say no when you might mean yes in twenty minutes.
- Don't count on a man to say anything other than yes when he
  means no.
- If you can't separate sexual need from whatever else you believe
  you need from a man, stay out of bed until you can't think about
  anything but sex. Then tell him you want him.
- Only tell him how to touch you when you badly want to be
  touched by him in just that way.

2 Manspeak—As She Rarely Hears It

• •

"What do I think is great sex? A woman with a talented tongue and a lot of time on her hands. I want her to swirl her tongue around my cock, paying special attention to the piss slit. Then move that tongue up and down the vein on the underside of the shaft. I want her to lick and suck me until there isn't a dry spot left on my cock and balls. I want pieces of my hair stuck between her teeth when I finally push her legs apart with my knees and relieve her with my toes."

—A twenty-nine-year-old systems-design analyst
from the Midwest

The sexual soundtrack in his head is not playing love songs. The words are dirty. The beat is hard. Imagine the Rolling Stones putting *Penthouse* to music, and you have his sexual voice as women seldom hear it. Women like to think the man who talks this way is a composite of every sweaty, grimy, high-school-dropout character who ever grunted his way through a B-movie. Wrong.

He is Everyman.

"It's the only way men knew how to talk sex until recent years," says a West Coast psychologist, age thirty-six. "Now many of us know the language for talking sensitively about sex to our women partners. We can say the words, with varying degrees of honesty and comfort. But I don't know a man, outside movies and novels, usually written by women, who can talk that way to other men. We simply do not sit around saying, 'The earth moved when I made love to my beloved last night.'

"The penis is never far from a man's thoughts. But he rarely talks about sex, the way women talk about sex, as the lovemaking which takes place between two people. He makes sex talk, which is about the graphic coming together of body parts. It is more like jock talk than anything women say."

Men make this "sex talk" to each other and to women they probably don't know. You've caught bits of these male exchanges spoken in low tones in public places, such as restaurants and bars, and at parties. "Look at the tits on her. I'd like to suck on one of those. Her nipples are hard. Go ahead, talk to her. She's creaming in her pants for you." You wrinkle your nose and walk quickly past.

Or, worse, you've been the object of manspeak on the street. "Hey, baby, looking good. . . . Baby, I could make you feel good too, give it to you like you've never had it, baby. You like 'em big, baby? I got one for you! Yeah!" Eyes either downcast or focused grimly ahead, you hurry by. You wonder what you've done wrong to encourage this unwanted attention. Skirt too short? Heels too high? Does your cleavage peek through the buttons on your blouse as you walk? You take it personally, but you shouldn't. There's nothing personal about the exchange. Manspeak is depersonalized talk.

Men toss these words into the fire merely to keep the flames burning. The words, like chunks of charcoal, bleak and cold, are not really thrown at a particular woman. They are fuel to stoke the fire in the furnace that keeps the penis going. Much of what men say to other men about women or call out to unknown women on the street is said to keep up the morale of the penis. Men sometimes ask:

Why can't women understand that men don't see them as individual people on the street?

"I worked construction jobs during the summers while I was going to college," says Jeff, thirty-three. "Some of the guys were laborers for life. Others were students or teachers who needed summer income. On the site, we were all the same. Cavemen. A bunch of guys scared of women and the sexual power they hold over us. A bunch of scared guys taking the offensive

to impress each other. Even if you didn't whistle or catcall, you pretended to be in on the game. None of them would have yelled out like that at a woman any of us had known."

Men rarely admit even to themselves that they sometimes resent the power women have over them. They are conditioned to control their feelings, and the intensity of desire, especially commingled with passionate love, is not so easily controlled. While we grew up on the myth of being swept away by a prince, they came of age under the burden of knowing they were expected to become the one who sweeps. We can faint, but they must remain strong, in control, to catch us. They also must wait for us to signal the onset of the romantic swoon before they can touch us. Sometimes their most strident, graphic street talk hides resentments and emotions they fear. The anonymous woman becomes the embodiment and target of their anger at that fear.

"I remember one time in my life when I was young and broke," writes a thirty-five-year-old engineer. "I worked at a laborer's job for a year to save enough money to finish college. I remember how angry I often was at the beautiful women who walked past without giving me a second glance. I was dirty. I smelled bad. The most important thing—I couldn't afford them. It shames me now to say this, but sometimes I called them 'cunt,' loud enough so they could hear me. I had a lot of anal-sex fantasies during that year. I wanted to shove it to them hard up their butts and make them like it. Young men who are broke feel a lot of anger at those beautiful sexy young women who are only interested in giving their favors to men who can afford them."

The tendency to become coarse and crude isn't limited to groups of blue-collar men. Normally articulate, courteous professionals behave in similar fashion. Yet the same men who can tell a stranger on the street what they'd like to do to her rarely talk to their best friends about the sex they're actually having with wives or girlfriends. Unlike women, they do not share intimate details with each other. Many of them find our willingness to do so embarrassing or appalling.

Men often ask:

Why don't women understand that sex is private?

"Some things are supposed to stay between a man and a woman. It bothers me when women talk. The first girl I was strongly attracted to in high school told several other girls about our first kiss. One of those girls told me. I still remember how embarrassed I felt. I never took that girl out again though I still wanted to touch her so bad it took my breath away. She wrote me a note apologizing, and I passed it around the room in math class. I wanted to burn her good. I still remember the feeling. In fact, I get twinges of it whenever I hear my wife nattering on the phone with some of her closest friends and I suspect the subject is sex, our sex," wrote a forty-year-old executive from the Midwest.

Men aren't comfortable talking about sex in the same personal yet detached way we do. We sometimes accuse them of having no feelings because they can't express them in a manner we find palatable. But they do have feelings. "God, do we have feelings. . . ." writes a graduate student in law. "Sometimes with women I feel the way a deaf person must feel trying to communicate with people who hear. One of us speaks with a mouth, the other with hands, and we can't understand each other."

If men have trouble communicating sexual feelings to us, they find it almost impossible to share them with male friends. They don't have that same comfortable place for sharing information, fears, and guilts. As young men, they brag and posture. As mature men, they observe a gentlemanly code of silence about the women they love. Other women, the ones they don't love, are reduced to the descriptive sum of body parts.

"What women often fail to understand is that [inexpressiveness] is not . . . stubbornness on the part of men," says Bernie Zilbergeld, nationally known clinical psychologist at the Human Sexuality Program, the University of California, San Francisco, in the book *Male Sexuality*. "We simply were not and are not given the permission to be expressive that most women were. We were not allowed to acknowledge even to ourselves all those emotions labeled unmanly, which has resulted in an inability to recognize and differentiate among them. . . . Talking about feelings . . . is considered feminine by the models we were raised on."

Men grew up believing that real men don't talk about sex the way women do. But they also learned at a reasonably young age that the women they cared about would expect them to say something. "You tell them what they want to hear," writes a twenty-six-year-old accountant. "And what they want to hear is love talk, not sex talk. You want sex. You talk love. Everybody's happy."

They ask this question about love lies:

Don't women know they make it necessary for men to lie to them?

"My number-one complaint about women and sex is they just can't let it be what it is. You don't always fall in love. I feel many women want to fall in love before they get close to a man. It's a catch-22. How do you fall in love unless you get close? How do you get close without sex? Unless a woman 'feels' for a guy, she won't decide to go to bed. So she lies to herself about the feelings. So he has to lie to her about his feelings. I love you, baby. I'll call you, baby. Yeah, Yeah, Yeah!" writes a New York computer analyst in his thirties.

Men aren't any more honest with women than we are with them. If we sometimes lie about wanting sex when we want love or material security, they sometimes lie about feeling love or at least the desire to see us again when they want, or only wanted, sexual release. A surprisingly large number of them think it's okay to tell us these three basic lies, because we "want" to hear them. The lies are: I'll call you. I love you. There's no one but you. Maybe men think the lies sound better than that lyric running through their minds, *I'd like to shove my cock inside you.* . . .

A woman's magazine editor recently told me, "Any issue with a cover line promising to explain why he didn't call when he said he would will sell a lot of copies. Women agonize over this issue, especially if they went to bed with him and *then* he didn't call."

"What are we supposed to say to a woman we've just fucked?" asked a dentist from the South. " 'Let's have lunch? Let's get together again soon?' Sometimes you have sex with a woman because you've let her think you're more interested than you are. And really you didn't know how interested you might be until after the sex. Maybe it wasn't that special, but you and she let it happen anyway. You probably won't call her again, because you won't feel a strong pull in her direction.

"Women like to make this out to be a conquest situation and damn the men for their conquest mentality—or else they beat themselves up for 'giving in' too soon. The thinking is, 'If I'd waited until the third date like they told me to do in *Glamour* magazine, he'd fall in love with me.' Not necessarily. Three dates or five or six doesn't guarantee things will get good between you. They invest the whole story with too much meaning. It was just sex. No woman wants to hear that, especially today when we're all supposed to be so much more careful than we have been. You lie. You say, 'I'll call you.' "

Some men even go so far as to say, "I love you" or "I think I'm falling in love with you," to get a woman into bed. Maybe they don't like themselves for doing it. Then they disappear because they're embarrassed. They think she believed every word and is now expecting a serious relationship to develop.

"I try to stay with 'I want you,' " explained a thirty-four-year-old lawyer from Tulsa. "It's honest. No, I take it back. Sometimes that isn't even completely honest. Men push for sex claiming we want it bad when sometimes we just want the physical closeness. You sound like a pussy telling a woman you want a cuddle."

Zilbergeld, in *Male Sexuality*, explains: "We tend to label any positive feelings we have toward another person as sexual. All of us—men, women, children—need support, validation, physical affection, tenderness, and the knowledge that we are loved and wanted. Sometimes these needs can best be met through sexual activity; many times they are best fulfilled in other ways. But since men were not taught to differentiate among these needs and since the needs themselves are suspect for us—is it really okay to want to be held or 'just' to snuggle or to want to hear that she cares for me? —whenever one of them presses for expression, we assume that sex is what we want. In sex we can get some of these other needs met without raising any questions about our masculinity."

Men identify all physical-intimacy needs as sexual. Sex is equated with that rock-hard penis always ready to perform. He can't get his needs met unless that penis *does* perform. Whatever he has to say to a woman to gain sexual access to her is justified by the requirements of the penis.

"You never tell a woman she isn't the only one," writes a salesman from the northeast. "They can't trust you and feel comfortable with you if they think they're being measured against the other woman or women in your life. It's a justifiable lie. It makes her feel good. It makes the sex good for her. You want it to be as good for her as it is for you, so you give it to her on her terms. Believe me, her terms are a lot more complicated than locating her clitoris."

How to Translate His Sex Talk

- Put more faith in what he does—like calling to make another date—than in what he says—like "I'll call you." (Your mother was right about this: Actions do speak louder than words.)
- Don't demand assurances of love or promises of calling. You'll get them—the assurances, that is. A cornered man will lie and feel justified in doing so.
- Remember, he isn't quite sure what you're saying either.

3 Nongender Speak: The Voice of Authority

....

"In the human male a sensation of ejaculatory inevitability develops for an instant immediately prior to, and then parallels in timing sequence, the first stage of the ejaculatory process (accessory-organ contractions). . . . This subjective experience of inevitability develops as seminal plasma is collecting in the prostatic urethra but before the actual emission of seminal fluid begins. The two-to-threefold distention of the urethral bulb developing in the terminal portions of the plateau phase also may contribute proprioceptively to the sensation of ejaculatory inevitability.

"During the second stage of the ejaculatory process (propulsion of seminal-fluid content from prostatic urethra to the urethral meatus) the male subjectively progresses through two phases: First, a contractile sensation is stimulated by regularly recurring contractions of the sphincter urethrae. Second, a specific appreciation of fluid volume develops as the seminal plasma is expelled under pressure along the lengthened and distended penile urethra."

—William H. Masters and Virginia E. Johnson describing the male orgasm in *Human Sexual Response*

"She was licking and biting and sucking me right out of my mind. The hot come was churning furiously in my balls. I couldn't stand it any longer, so I shot my copious load down her throat."

—A letter from a *Forum* reader on one of his orgasms

The first descriptive passage could be printed on back of a church bulletin without upsetting any but the most dogged of readers, for only they would make it to the end with both mental alertness and comprehensive powers undulled. Masters and Johnson may be the worst best-selling writers in the world. That no one could find their material pruriently entertaining helped make sex therapy more acceptable than sex itself. The sex therapist–authors who followed the famous team write in more accessible prose, but theirs is still the voice of nongender speak, a voice more closely aligned to womanspeak than manspeak. It talks about feelings though it doesn't express them.

In 1978, I interviewed Masters and Johnson at the institute in St. Louis for a story on sex therapy in *St. Louis* magazine. In the earlier days of therapy, they told me, the number-one presenting problem had been premature ejaculation. By that time PE and other "dysfunctions" caused, they said, by "lack of information" and "easily cured by simple physical techniques" had been replaced by lack of desire of one or both partners. Today, more than a decade later, inhibited-desire syndrome, is still categorized as the number-one problem.

Their work, which bore the stamp of both names equally, was said to have been, for several years at least, primarily directed by Masters. Johnson earned her doctorate years after her partner. After meeting her, I certainly didn't doubt either her intelligence or her influence on Masters. But their professional equality was a feminist statement that set the philosophical tone for a treatment movement, and the tone had a female bias. They were compensating women who'd been categorized as frigid because no one had told them about the clitoris.

Nearly all the early practitioners of sex therapy were trained at the Masters and Johnson Institute. As these therapists—including Lonnie Barbach, Eve Margolies, and others—achieved recognition on their own, they also wrote books that focused on the historically neglected female orgasm and its infinite possibility. They wrote in nongender speak, setting down explanations and instructions that opened up a new erotic world for women.

This voice of authority quickly became the voice we respect when the subject is sex. The reasons are obvious.

THE NEUTRAL VOICE IN THE WAR BETWEEN THE SEXES

First, men and women don't speak the same language when the subject is sex. The nongender voice is accessible to both sexes and can be used without getting anyone excited or embarrassed. As a tool for discussing sexual problems or imparting new information, it is outstanding. In bed, the language is a little too serious and tense for pillow talk.

"It's easier for a woman to say 'clitoral stimulation' than to tell you how she'd like to be touched and how good it feels when you do," writes a Chicago office manager. "But I'd rather hear her talk dirty. As soon as I hear that phrase 'clitoral stimulation' coming from a woman's lips, I feel lectured."

Second, the neutral voice makes our fears seem more manageable. We accept that women fear men, who have, or are perceived to have, physical, political, and financial power over us. We fail to accept that men fear women. According to Zilbergeld, "Female sexuality has been a particularly vexing area for men, who have believed and vainly tried to reconcile many outlandish and contradictory ideas about how women related to sex. . . . Ignorance breeds doubt and fear, and to these emotions must be added others—envy and anger."

The voice of authority imparts knowledge, which helps to quell everyone's fears—though it may have inadvertently incited increased male envy and anger. "My girl believes anything she reads about men and sex, as long as it's written in an authoritative tone, and preferably written by a woman," writes a graduate student. "I read her a man's letter in *Penthouse*, which I thought perfectly expressed my own erotic sensations on having a blow job performed. She said real men don't think like that, only those subhumans who write letters to sex magazines."

Third, this language makes sex more socially acceptable as a topic for books, magazine articles, and talk shows. (Does the fact that women are the primary consumers of these media forms further influence the female orientation of the language or merely encourage its rapid spread?) Before Masters and Johnson, women talked in code about "down there," "that time of the month," "in the family way," and his "thing." The word "pregnancy" couldn't be used on TV in the Fifties when Lucille Ball was expecting little Ricky.

Finally, nongender speak gives an acceptable voice to feelings. It is now possible for the articulate man to discuss his sexual feelings with some equanimity. The new language upgraded female feelings from the level of the pulp-romance dialogue to ruminations worthy of psychological literature. It also gave women, more comfortable with feelings anyway, the communication edge.

INCREASING THE DECIBLE LEVEL OF THE EXPERT VOICE

"The G-spot was the last straw for me. Look, I care about pleasing a woman. I don't understand why the site of her orgasms has to change every few years like her hemlines," writes a thirty-seven-year-old salesman.

This new language for talking about sex led to an explosion of information and some changes in our collective sexual thinking. For instance, few people still regard the simultaneous orgasm as the ultimate, or even attainable, erotic experience. Most men know that most women need some form of clitoral stimulation to reach orgasm. A minority of women will reach orgasm through intercourse alone. Men may not like it that their partners are not among this minority. Some may convince themselves their women do have orgasms through intercourse, but most accept the fact that some form of stimulation other than, or in addition to, intercourse is needed. They and we have come to regard orgasm as a separate but equal proposition. First her turn, then his.

"A gentleman makes every effort to be sure his partner has had a climax before he lets go," writes a man in Cleveland who speaks for many others. "That is the most difficult part of sex, especially with a new partner. You don't want to get so hard into it you forget your manners in her regard."

Clearly, the voice of authority has been heard. Sadly, we've had to pay a price for the word. In *Re-making Love*, Ehrenreich, Hess, and Jacobs say, "The experts had consumed themselves with methods to hold men back or speed women along. . . . Sex was becoming more like jogging: It was better at one's own pace. . . . *How to Make Love to a Man*, by Alexandra Penny, expressed, more than any other manual, the growing physical alienation between heterosexuals. It was so difficult for men and women to satisfy each other simultaneously that Penny advised them to take turns, not during the same evening but alternately, with the woman giving the man whatever he wants one night and the man reciprocating on a separate occasion. . . . This was theatrical sex, so tightly scripted that there was little room for spontaneous heterosexual impulses to destroy a scene."

There was even less room for the male sexual voice, deemed harsh, vulgar, crude, and technically imprecise. Women really didn't want to hear men describe their own orgasmic experiences, share in graphic detail their fantasies, or worse, tell the truth about what turns them on.

THE CENSORING OF MANSPEAK

"*I am so tired of women lecturing me on the evils of porn,*" writes a TV producer, age forty-one. "*Yes, I like the nudes in* Playboy *and* Penthouse. *Yes, I like to read the letters. I'm not turned on by violence, whether it's against women or against men or against lab rats. Why do these women equate an airbrushed nude layout with the whips-and-chains torture stuff? It's not the same. I never thought I'd live to be this old still hiding my magazines under my bed.*"

Our distrust of any but the expert voice only partially explains why manspeak is deemed the least worthy of the three voices. Its graphic, urgent vocabulary is the verbal equivalent of dirty pictures, the soundtrack of pornography, the male voice at its most strident. After a brief period when pornography was so socially acceptable that Jackie Onassis was reported in the gossip columns to have been seen leaving a showing of *Deep Throat*, a coalition of right-wing politicians, religious leaders, and feminists came down against it, in the name of God and women's rights.

Negative stereotyping of the male proliferated. In a *Ms.* magazine editorial, Gloria Steinam said, after detailing the evils of child pornography: "But how different are those obsessed, power-hungry purchasers of child pornography from the many 'normal' men who are convinced of the need and permission to be violent, to conquer sexually?" Similar expressions of the belief that "All men are rapists" were repeated regularly in *Ms.* and more mainstream publications.

If women don't need pornographic images for arousal, feminist leaders reasoned, why should men? The antiporn movement lumps together everything from *Penthouse* to kiddie porn and snuff films in one category. Their position, a political version of the squeeze technique for the brain instead of the penis, more vigorously than sex therapy seeks to remake male sexuality in more acceptable, more *female* terms. They simply refuse to accept the differing sexual biology of the male.

Pornography has been blamed for everything from creating a climate in which sexual harassment or violence against women is favorably regarded or tolerated, to inciting men to rape. While porn is the identified target, the real object of attack is male sexuality. The male nudes in *Playgirl* or the jockstrap-clad dancers of the Chippendales are acceptable and amusing entertainment because they are entertainment for women. If we enjoy male nudity, we're liberated; when they enjoy female nudity, they're sexist pigs.

"Male sexual passion has become sinful again," writes Alan Bloom in *The Closing of the American Mind*, "because it culminates in 'sexism.' Women, it is said, are made into objects, they are raped by their husbands as well as by strangers, they are sexually harassed by professors and employers at school and at work. All these crimes must be legislated against and punished. What sensitive male can avoid realizing how dangerous his sexual passion is?"

The feminists are really against pornography, he says, because "it is a reminiscence of the old love relationship, which involved differentiated sexual roles—roles now interpreted as bondage and domination. Pornography caters to and encourages the longing men have for women and its unrestrained satisfaction. This is what feminist anti-pornographers are against, not the debasement of sentiment or the threat to the family. And this is why they exempt homosexual pornography from censorship, for it is by definition not an accomplice to the male-female tyranny and even helps to undermine it."

Who can blame a man for feeling under attack when his sexual nature is deemed base, his partner can pinpoint his dysfunctions and outline a cure in precise therapese, and any list of nonfiction best-sellers includes at least one book on what's wrong with him emotionally? His voice has been drowned out by womanspeak and nongender speak, the voice of authority. Women don't want to hear him speak unless it's from a script prepared for an Alan Alda character in a film.

In "Stop Blaming Men for Everything!", an article in the August 1989 issue of *Mademoiselle*, Alex Heard said something that struck me as a warning shot over the bow of our boat: "Many men *are* bad, but we're not all testosterone-crazed lab monkeys who must be retrained before we're fit to be voltage-prodded down the wedding aisle."

Suggestions for Handling Sex Books and Articles in the Expert Voice

- Do not quote directly from them to your man, especially just before, during, or after sex.
- Don't suggest he should read your sex guides because he might "learn something."
- Don't keep them in the bedroom.
- Buy books and read articles that tell you what you can do for yourself to make sex more enjoyable or how to be more accepting of your own, or his, sexuality.

Part Two

SEDUCTION: WHO HAS SEX WITH WHOM AND WHEN

The Mystery of Desire

•••

"In truth, desire is a mysterious human riddle that has always wanted satisfactory definition."
—F. Gonzalez-Crussi, *On the Nature of Things Erotic*

Until modern times, seduction was controlled by the man and fraught with moral peril for both partners if he won the consent of the woman he desired. That so much rested on the outcome invested the pursuit with an excitement not easily matched in post—sexual revolutionary America where seduction is expected to lead directly into the beginning of a *relationship*. What a solid, serious, responsible, and dull word that has become! Look what Lancelot and Guinevere did to Camelot. Can you imagine a *relationship* wreaking such havoc on a world? Now their love affair would be tolerated until it had played its course with none of the principals missing a state appearance.

Today the seduction is generally conceded to be the first time you and he have sex, or to a lesser extent, anytime one person coerces the less willing other into having sex, especially to "revitalize" a flagging sexual relationship. We often seduce him, or more likely, allow ourselves to be seduced, because it is time to move the relationship along. Women still worry about when to have sex for the first time, because we believe it is a determining factor in whether a man will, or will not, choose to commit. And we worry about being the initiator, the seducer. Apparently we should take on this role with caution. Though the number-one complaint expressed about women by 80 percent of the men in my survey was our passivity in bed, they also described the sexually aggressive woman, the one who makes the *first* move, in distinctly predatory terms.

The sexual revolution left us with the myth of a man who was

ever ready and a woman who was ever available—and thus no comfortable explanation for their failure to desire each other. *She is not
appealing. He is not a real man.* Finding neither a palatable excuse,
she devours advice on how to dress seductively and schedules sexual
interludes with her man. If that fails, she blames him, and/or he
looks elsewhere.

By the time that revolution sighed to a climax, we had thrilled
to the daytime talk-show tales of forbidden love finally realized
between women and their fathers-in-law, men and their children's
baby-sitters, cross-dressers and their ordinary, rather frumpy wives,
and even, God would have previously forbid, lesbian nuns. There
was no passionate, preferably monogamous, union left unexplored
by Phil or Oprah. No coupling was too awful to contemplate, and
no seduction that could not be planned.

But we were left with a new disorder, inhibited-desire syndrome,
sometimes blamed on the women's movement, and most often il-
lustrated by the yuppie couple whining about lack of time—for
anything but the making, counting, and spending of money. Did
they eroticize greed because money was harder to get, and thus more
romantic, than sex? While desire remains elusive, seduction, or so
we believe, can be explained, orchestrated, and accomplished when
necessary by following basic steps. If you do the right things, you
can make sex happen.

We believe seduction can successfully occur whenever we choose
because a man, of course, is *always* up for sex, whether he's really
interested or not. Or, as Barry McCarthy says in *Male Sexual Awareness*, "Strong sexual desire is viewed as a natural characteristic of
male sexuality and as a measure of masculinity." If desire wanes,
someone must be to blame for the somnolent state of the penis.
"Most men blame desire problems on some outside source (their
job, their spouse's weight, lack of time, sex's becoming routine,
etc.) and believe they need a 'magic pill' or an outside source (a
twenty-year-old sexy woman) to regain desire. It's as if desire isn't
a personal part of the man but is controlled from external sources
or the cultural stereotype of masculinity."

"Desire is a wondrous, serendipitous event," says my friend Jeff, who, at forty-two, recently left his wife of twenty years for the magic pill of another woman. Once a witty master of the double entendre, he now waxes eloquent on what it is he desires in a woman, or *from* her, now that he does so avidly desire her. (His effusions, more often than not, inspire in me the "yuck" response, though I am envious of his blind happiness, temporary state that I know it to be.) "There is no planned seduction, no power struggle," he lectures, "in the natural coming together of two people when the time is right for them to be together."

Jeff and his discovery of soulful sex notwithstanding, men still equate desire with lust—the physical, and sometimes accompanying emotional, need to get inside the woman they want. Maybe they don't understand why, but they know they want possession, physical possession of her, for a limited but intense duration. Inside her, they hope to lose themselves and find themselves accepted and validated, all at the same time. The truth is perhaps too frightening and overwhelming for us to acknowledge it in any but mechanical or sentimental terms.

The feeling is elusive, and not guaranteed to last the life of a relationship. In some cultures, however, this fact is accepted with equanimity. Chortling as he spoke, a Frenchman recently told me, "You Americans are so innocent—shocked when people grow old and die, even more shocked when [sexual] desire does so. You think you are entitled to the rebirth [of lust], not blessed when it does occur."

4 The Sexual Setting

••

"She invited me in; and I knew she was going to seduce me. I had seen the sexy lingerie peeking between the buttons of her dress-for-success blouse at dinner. She'd been sending the signals, and I'd been returning them. Her apartment was set for soft light at the touch of the switch by the door. Everything was soft, overstuffed and pillowed, and printed in tiny patterns, tastefully feminine. She had plants, healthy plants, always a good sign in a woman. She kicked off her shoes, shrugged out of her jacket, and told me to sit down while she poured the wine. I sat on the sofa and picked up a magazine. Roseanne Barr, that man-hating bitch, was on the cover. I asked myself, Did it mean anything that she was smirking there on the coffee table in this sexy woman's living room?"

—A magazine editor who lives in Chicago

This man's story exemplifies two truisms about female seduction strategies: They are as obvious as the lace teddy showing through your starched white shirt; and the best-laid plan can be subverted by the intrusion of the outside world. Obviousness is not necessarily bad. (The Chicago editor was pleased and flattered by her attention to the small details she considered seductive.) Whether for bad or good, the world will intrude. (Fortunately, he reports, he was able to put Roseanne, who for him symbolizes female rage at men, facedown on the floor and kick her under the sofa.) And sometimes men, like women, will latch upon the smallest jarring detail as an excuse for opting out. ("Then I noticed she . . ." smoked, chewed gum, had bad teeth, heavy thighs, skinny legs, a mole on her left nipple, and on and on.)

The perfect setting for sex, like perfect bodies and perfect sex, only exists on a movie screen. Most men say they prefer her home, dimly lit, but no bedside candles please. Don't come on to him at the office. In fact, restrict your movements to lightly flirtatious ones in public.

The exactly right moment for seduction is an invention of the marriage-guide authors, but most men want to make the first move the first time and *not* on the first date. Sleeping with him on the first date, however, won't kill the possibility of a relationship developing if that possibility really existed in the first place. Women rarely think he wouldn't have called back anyway. We're only too eager to blame the silent phone on Having Sex Too Soon. Repeatedly, men tell me we're wrong.

Perhaps they want to control the seduction because they don't know how to say no to an attractive woman. One of the questions asked of the men I surveyed was: "Do you believe a real man should always want sex with an attractive woman?" More than three-fourths of the respondents—a geographic, racial, and religious background mix representing income levels of under $10,000 and over $100,000—answered yes. One man wrote, "Yes, I can't shake that belief even though I know it's foolish." And 85 percent, obviously including many men who responded negatively to the first question, said yes to the follow-up: "Do you believe the same man should always be able to perform with an attractive woman?"

In the beginning, be indirect rather than direct. He knows what you're doing, especially if you're doing it on the third date, generally regarded as the acceptable date for first sex. But he wants the planning to be nearly invisible, like the skeleton inside the body. ("I like it when a woman seduces me, when I feel desire emanating from her, like heat waves from the center," says a Georgia merchant.)

Men do know when they're being seduced. If anything, rather failing to detect genuine female interest in them, they will assume her desire for sex on the basis of that glimpse of lingerie and the softness of her sofa pillows. ("Why do women escalate the flirtation when I fail to respond?" a Texan asks. "I'm not sexually deaf. You don't have to yell because I'm tactfully ignoring what I've chosen not to hear.") The majority of men will succumb to the seduction, allowing themselves to be sexually led—even if they later feel used.

("I was engaged in postorgasmic chitchat with a woman who had all but dragged me into her bed. She kidded me about 'using and abusing me,' but hell, I felt used!") Maybe they say they'd rather be seduced at her place because it's the easiest place to avoid being if they don't want sex with her.

They ask:

Why can't I refuse a willing female without feeling guilty?

"I know it doesn't make good sense, but I feel like less of a man if I don't respond to an opportunity to have sex with an attractive woman. The exception, of course, would be a client who throws herself at me in the office, which has happened several times over the years. Women going through a divorce are dangerous, especially if their husbands' affairs have been part of the problem. I classify that as a direct proposition, different from a seduction, which can be either the culmination of a long flirting process or something akin to spontaneous combustion in the body of one who successfully transmits the spark to the other. Do you think I'm going overboard in defining seduction as a way of explaining why I can turn down a direct hit from a stranger without feeling guilty?" writes a Cleveland attorney.

Men think they need a very good reason to reject the sexual advances of a woman. They shared their stories of turning down direct propositions from "horny" female co-workers, wives, or girlfriends of brothers or friends, or their own wives' or girlfriends' friends. Rarely did they confess saying no to a woman they had no good *nonsexual* reason for refusing.

"It's acceptable to say no if a higher loyalty dictates that you don't do anything with this woman," explains a plumbing contractor from the south. "Otherwise, you feel like a pussy."

Spurned women, they say, can quite cruelly reinforce the feeling.

"A woman in my office was pursuing me," writes a corporate communications director from the Midwest. "It wasn't my imagination. Other people were picking up on it and kidding me about it. She is pretty and bright, but I'm not sexually attracted to her. I declined her repeated invitations for drinks after work, ignored her comments about my sexy body, and gently moved away from her when she 'casually' touched me. One day she asked me why I was so afraid of emotional involvement with a woman who is my equal. Where does a woman get off making that kind of sweeping judgment on the basis of a man's disinclination to fuck her? Later I heard she'd been telling people she thought I was either a misogynist or gay. If a woman doesn't want me, I figure she doesn't want me. I don't read her psychological history into it. To be fair, I guess men do that when they accuse a woman who turns them down of being frigid or a cock tease."

And a graduate student writes that a spurned woman's anger makes him mad: "It pisses me off that a woman thinks her sexual overtures will always be greeted with enthusiasm. Mine aren't!"

As women have become more sexually assertive, men have begun to chafe under the constraints of the machismo code. It was easier to pretend they were always ready for sex if they were the only sex permitted to initiate it. Lack of desire could be rationalized as "too much respect for her." Now they have no easy explanation, and that makes them angry.

Their anger, however, is more likely to be directed at us than at the code. Our anger when desire flags and seductive ploys fail is also more likely to be directed at them than at the code. We don't question where we got the idea that any man we want should want us, do we? It's the machisma code: *Any man I desire should desire me—unless I am undesirable or there is something wrong with him.*

Maybe that is why many of us, male and female, frequently cite minor physical details as justification for saying no. Men ask:

Don't women know how critical little details can be?

"I like it when a woman makes a move on me, even the first move, as long as she wants sex and not to prove something through sex. A lot of angry women dress and act seductively. Sexual vampires. I remember a woman I met at a party. Very sexy. Long red fingernails, probably fake. I imagined her raking those fingernails down my back, and it turned me on. I offered her a ride home, and she accepted. She was a chain-smoker. One hand on my thigh, the nails running up and down, dangerously close to my manhood, the other hand wrapped around a cigarette. Those long red nails flicking cigarette ashes out my window turned me off. The same image can go from sexy to scary with the slightest little twist. There was something

so hostile in the way she held those cigarettes. I dropped her off. I never called her," writes an advertising copywriter.

Once again, a man was describing a woman's seductive behavior as angry, threatening, dangerous, and scary. Some men sense anger in the sexually aggressive woman as she's making the initial seductive ploy. They feel she's demanding their cooperation rather than eliciting it. What she wants from them is more than sex, they say. Whether they respond to her or not, they resent her for taking something they didn't mean to give—or taking it before they had a chance to give it.

"Retribution, maybe. Retribution for what another man, or several men, have put her through," one man speculates. "She wants to have your balls in her trophy case." Another says: "She woke up one morning, decided she was ready for marriage and a child, and you're just the guy to give them to her. Is she pissed off if you have your own agenda!"

Are they behaving like defensive males who can't come to terms with their own sexual disinterest in a particular woman in whom they believe they should have interest, or do they have a point to make about anger as a seductive force in women?

Not surprisingly, they most often report sensing that anger in women who are making the first move on men they don't know very well. On the other hand, after the first time or two, they wish women would initiate sex more often. A telephone repairman from the northeast writes: "I wish the women in my life would have taken the lead more often. I would like to see somewhat of a balance. I hate always having to initiate sex. What's even worse is trying to initiate sex and getting denied, especially if you've only had sex once or twice with her before. Has she written you off as lacking potential?

"I was in bed with a woman last week. She said to me, 'I'm glad you invited yourself in tonight, or we wouldn't be here like this.' I said, 'You mean if I had said good night at the door, you'd have let it go at that?' She said that she was very horny but couldn't bring herself to ask me if I wanted to spend the night with her. This wasn't the first night I had sex with her. We'd been doing this for over a year. She said that she was afraid that I would say no, and she doesn't take rejection well. 'What about men,' I said, 'don't you think we have a difficult time dealing with it too?' "

Being seduced, even ravished by an attractive woman, is a favorite male fantasy—but like the female rape fantasy, it can be misleading. Women don't want rape. We want to be swept away by desire so strong it negates our inhibitions and guilts. Men want to be taken—when they're ready to be taken. Otherwise, they feel set up for possible performance failure.

"The best lover I ever had," says an Indiana executive, "was a very seductive woman, a very active sex partner. She paid close attention to my moods. If she could sense I was too tired, she wouldn't put me on the spot. She'd give me a back rub or let me rest my head in her lap so she could stroke my temples until I fell asleep. Naturally, if I revived, I was in a good position to change my mind.".

Sometimes a man decides the timing was off—in retrospect. He is that man in whose brain the macho code is most deeply embedded. After virtually mounting an irresistible erotic assault to your inhibitions, he *really* doesn't respect you in the morning. You can't identify him with 100 percent accuracy in advance, because he transcends types. Latin descent and/or a Catholic-school background are frequently associated with the breed. He may, however, have blond hair, a name like Skip, and a family bench in the Anglican Church.

"Recently I was with a woman I genuinely liked," Carlos says. "I kept escalating the erotic attention because she let me. At what point am I expected to be able to stop myself if she won't stop me? Soon we were in bed. It was very good, but when it was over, I was sorry she'd let me have her so soon. Yes, I know it takes two to tango. Women have told me I shouldn't be so insistent if I am secretly hoping they will refuse. I know I shouldn't be. I am."

What you shouldn't be is worried about what he thinks. Regard the experience as one night of crazed passion—and move on. Most men believe our fear of negative judgments holds us back sexually. And many think we work too hard at being seductive. They ask:

Why do women try so hard to be sexy?

"I am seduced by a woman's clothing first. If her clothes look like they suit her body and personality—and you can see she has a body under them—she has sex appeal. Personal style is sexy. A woman doesn't have to be a size two to have style. Then, if she kisses well and responds warmly to my kisses and caresses, I'm hers if she wants me," writes a St. Louis contractor.

What a woman wears and how much warmth she projects are more important than seductive techniques. ("Attitude is everything.") Over 60 percent of the men in my survey rated sexy lingerie a turn-on. ("I love it when you can catch a hint of lace, if only the texture of it beneath her blouse.") The clothing worn over that underwear should be subtly sexy rather than blatantly so. ("I'm not comfortable with women who could be confused with the hookers if they wandered into the wrong neighborhood.") While some men must fail to respond to a pair of legs in sheer black stockings, they haven't been in touch with me.

"Women in New York City wear a lot of black stockings and high heels with their career clothes," says a Wall Street broker. "They have got to be the sexiest women in the world. I don't know how they do it, but they look smart, powerful, *and* sexy. Even the secretaries have that 'Don't fuck with me' look playing simultaneously with their 'But wouldn't you love to?' eyes.

"The most seductive thing New York women do is cross and recross their legs while they're having drinks or dinner with you. If she crosses her legs many times in the course of the evening, she's coming on to you. Only a few times? She's just shifting positions for comfort."

Men do focus on the small behavior details, reading in them the signals that indicate likely acceptance or refusal of sexual overtures. If she leans toward him while talking, perhaps affording glimpses of cleavage, she's interested. If her response to light touches on the hand, arm, shoulders is to return the touch or lean into it, she's interested. If she moves away, she's not.

"A woman is being seductive when she accepts and returns your touches while making eye contact," a Philadelphian writes. "She has a frankly interested look in her eyes. Women can do that without seeming to leer better than men can. In fact, women seduce with their eyes.

"I can look into a woman's eyes and read her attitudes about men—whether she likes or trusts us—and know if she's going to be good in bed or not. Women who like men are better lovers than women who don't—no matter how much they practice sucking on green bananas to get it right."

Interestingly, the best way to seduce him is *not* to give him a physical facsimile of the girl of his X-rated dreams.

"Women who make it a point to find out how you like a woman to dress and behave sexy on the first date and present themselves that way on the second date turn me off," says Michael. "On the first date with Irene, whom I found very attractive, I shared my fantasies of wanting to date a woman who would meet me at a bar wearing a short tight dress, garter belt and stockings, and no other underwear. She would be drenched in my favorite perfume, Shalimar, which, by the way, wasn't Irene's perfume until the next time I saw her. She was drenched in the stuff and wearing a short tight dress. I sat on the bar stool and she whispered in my ear, 'I'm not wearing any underwear.' Then she licked my ear, which normally drives me wild.

"I felt like a cornered rat. I told her something unexpected had come up at the office and I only had time for a quick drink. I never saw her again. She was trying too damned hard. You know, if she'd done that after I'd known her awhile, it would have been heaven."

All You Ever Need to Know About Seductive Behavior

- You might copy details from a fashion layout, but not the whole look. In the same way, pick and choose among the hints you read for dressing, walking, talking sexy. Add new little details to your own personal style. Don't scrap it in favor of someone else's.
- Trying too hard is the cardinal sin.

- Listen to your body and his. Maybe you decided tonight's the night for reasons that have nothing to do with desire. Maybe you should reconsider.
- Remember, he has the right to say no. But don't let a refusal crush you.

5 The Sexual Players

●●●

"The seduction phase of a relationship is the most interesting part—and not only because it gets you laid. You learn almost everything you need to know about a woman from how she acts before and after sex. In the heat of fucking, I'm not a good observer. Afterward, I know if she's the type to give it all away because she's given her body to me: multiple contented sighs in direct proportion to orgasmic twitches she probably faked; dewy-eyed, meaningful soul-searching looks; suggests next encounter before my cock is dry. Or, if she's going to use sex as a reward or withhold it as a punishment: never praises my performance lavishly; asks many questions about hers, meant to gauge her impact on me; requests a glass of wine or cup of hot tea, even though it's her apartment. Or, if she can fuck her brains out and still get out of bed as the same person she was climbing in: she will be tender and affectionate, but not gooey. She will probably want to talk, which is great, because she won't want to talk about sex or relationships. While she's stroking my head, she'll ask me about what I was like as a little boy or where I was when Kennedy was shot."

—A company president from the Midwest

Seduction has always been a game of sexual power in which the distribution of power depends largely on the status of the players. The end result was inevitably a redistribution of the chips usually in his favor, even though he started out ahead anyway. Until recently only men had the prerogative of choosing a much younger partner, or someone from a lower socioeconomic group. Women married, or slept, up; men, down. Women lost something by "giving in," while men gained whatever it was we lost. They had the double edge; we had the double standard. All that has changed somewhat. Perhaps part of the confusion modern men feel about such gender issues as role reversals and bedroom equality is rooted in this new distribution of power.

The power shifts—and shifts dramatically—in the game of seduction depending initially on what the players bring to the game and then on how they handle their power. The main factors influencing the balance are: age, marital status, social class, and vulnerability. The edge usually goes to the older partner, the married lover in an affair between a cheating spouse and a single person, the one whose social, especially economic, status is higher, and the least emotionally vulnerable of the two.

Women have sex with younger men and those who make far less money. Female executives sleep with male chauffeurs. Sometimes the woman and not the man has had more sexual experience. In many cases, men are handling the new power division quite well.

"My lover has a college degree and I don't," writes a Mississippi laborer. "She's ten years older than I am and more experienced. I've learned a lot from her, sexually and otherwise. I don't feel less a man for that."

Other men may retreat into passive behavior: "Early on she took charge," says a young video technician. "I let her because she was ahead of me in years, income, experience. She called me for dates. I wouldn't call her. It drove her nuts. She said, 'I know you want to see me because you always say yes. Why don't you ever call?' I couldn't give her an answer."

Or they may abruptly drop out of these new relationships without explaining why. We call them hit-and-run lovers or Don Juans. Sometimes he's none of the above, only scared. This is often true of the emotionally vulnerable male, the man who has recently and/ or unhappily become "single" again.

"The first time after my divorce that I had sex with a woman who truly moved me, I panicked," John says. "I was scared to let myself be open for pain again. I left in the morning while she was sleeping, and I didn't call her again. I convinced myself there was something untrustworthy about her. Women don't have any idea how much power they have over men. A year later, I still think about that woman. I don't have the nerve to call her now. It's been too long. She probably thinks I'm a jerk, if she ever thinks of me at all."

Or, she pushes him to wrest control from her, in some way. Who can't cite a relationship in which an economically and socially powerful woman has given all her power away to a man—because *she* couldn't accept his being in the position she, or both, perceived as inferior?

"I just came out of the worst relationship of my life," writes a painter from the northeast. "I loved this woman, but I treated her badly. She almost begged me to. When we met, I had just lost my business. She had been made vice-president of her firm. On our first date, she minimized herself and her accomplishments. I saw that as both an indication of her weakness and her low opinion of me. We entered into a love-hate relationship with periodic bouts of wild, violent sex.

"We equalized the power through sex. I spanked her first with my hand, then my belt. I never broke the skin, but I got to the point where I couldn't get excited with her until I'd spanked her. Toward the end I wouldn't fuck her any way but anally. I lied to her, cheated on her, and told her she was a lousy lay. Finally, she walked. You know what? I wish she would have stopped me before it was too late. I couldn't stop myself."

Men often ask:

Why do women give so much away so soon?

"In the beginning of any relationship, women have all the power. A man is worried if he will get laid—and that's all up to her. When he does get laid, he's worried if he'll get laid regularly—and that's all up to her. When he's getting laid regularly, he's wondering if he'll get laid the way he wants to get laid—and that's really all up to her. When he gets that, he starts taking her for granted, because she lets him. She hands over the keys," writes a twenty-seven-year-old Philadelphian.

Over the years many men have told me stories with a similar theme: Once a sexual relationship is well established, the woman, who had the control until that point, suddenly forfeits it. They aren't sure why she does it. Sometimes, they aren't even aware of how she does it. They're positive, however, that *she* does.

"Men are blamed for losing interest in a woman once they know they can have her," says Gene, twenty-nine. "I don't get bored with a woman because I feel reasonably certain she'll have sex with me since she's been doing it on a fairly regular basis. I get bored because she changes into someone who isn't as interesting now. She lets me take advantage in little ways, like being late without calling. Maybe women think they have more invested in sexual relationships than men do. Maybe they think they can hold on by giving in on non-sexual points."

Everyone admits that keeping a relationship on an equal power basis is difficult. "Somebody always needs or loves a little more," says a Chicago banker, "but in a good relationship, it isn't always the same somebody. The need shifts." He also concedes that women have to fight their social conditioning to surrender, submit, relinquish control outside the bedroom as well as inside.

"This is pure speculation," says a forty-five-year-old Florida real-estate broker, "but maybe women give up control because they've been conditioned to believe that surrender is the price women pay for having sex. I've had many relationships over the last twenty-five years, with women of all ages, and for the most part, I've found them incapable of enjoying sex without brainwashing themselves into believing they're in love."

By surrendering control, he means "giving away too much of herself. She will adjust her schedule to suit mine, learn to eat sushi because I like sushi, and in extreme cases, adopt my personal tastes regarding music, movies, and sports and assume my political opinions as her own. All that—just because we're fucking."

And another man says: "They don't so much give up the power in a relationship. Rather, they dump the responsibility for their lives on you, and mask it as giving something away. All they're giving away is responsibility for themselves they don't want to have anymore."

Some men believe the power imbalance is more likely to occur among the traditional couples, of older man, younger woman; richer man, poorer woman—especially if the man is much older or richer. In more nontraditional couplings, the woman may start out with enough power chips to make her come out equal even after giving several of them away to her man. There are hidden references to power as these men describe why they like women of different ages:

"Younger women aren't set in their thought processes," a forty-four-year-old divorced professor said, in explaining why he seldom dates anyone over thirty-five. "They aren't sure they know the one and only right way for everything, from the right time to have a baby to whether your shirts should come back from the laundry on a hanger or in a box. I can't get it up around these know-it-all women. That's the plain and simple truth. Their obsessive lecturing beats me down."

"Women over thirty-five make the best lovers," says a twenty-two-year-old truck driver. "They know how to be seductive without being coy. They give everything they promise in bed—and more. Maybe they need younger men. They're probably too much for guys their age."

Aside from Kinsey, who drew several correlations between social class and sexual behavior, the experts shy away from the subject. Kinsey found that the lower classes had intercourse sooner, cheated on their marriages faster, and engaged in less foreplay than the upper classes. Today, he would probably find fewer differences in sexual behavior between the classes and more cross-class sexual pairings in which other factors influence the sex. Perhaps he would choose to focus on the power balance.

"I was married to a woman who suddenly began earning a lot more money than I did," says a Georgia postal worker. "It wrecked our marriage, especially the sex part. I can't blame everything on her. She didn't emasculate me. Money emasculated me."

"I dated a white woman," says Miguel, a New Yorker of Puerto Rican descent. "I loved making love to this woman. But we ran into all kinds of cultural difference problems. I wanted her to play a little hard to get, and she put this priority on honesty and openness and admitting her needs and desires. She hated 'games,' but I know how to play them well. I think she liked me as a person, with no thought to my skin color. When we were out together, I would see us the way other people saw us, a white woman with a 'Rican man. I thought the white man would look at us and think, Oh, yeah, those Latinos, they have the gonads to last all night. I didn't like feeling that way, like her lower-class stud."

Perhaps a forty-five-year-old investment broker gets closest to the bone with his analysis of sex and power: "I am a black man, and I find being with black women my own age an uncomfortable experience. They're mad as hell. They aren't going to take it anymore. And they let me know that, first thing out of the box. Now these women have a lot of legitimate gripes about how the world has treated them . . . but I'm not the world.

"With younger black women or white or Asian women of any age, I don't run into that rage directed at the black man. They aren't trying to wrest control of the relationship from me. Women under thirty aren't so mad. And white women see me as someone who's had to work harder to get anywhere within the white male establishment, as they have. We have an immediate bond. They're mad at the older white guys, not at me."

Part of a woman's sexual appeal to a man is the power she has or doesn't have. He may be attracted only to a strong woman or a weak one—or a strong woman he can bring to her knees. Her odds of appealing to him if she isn't his power type are slight.

"It's not that she did anything wrong or could have done something else right," Miguel explains. "She represented to me a situation I couldn't control, and I didn't like it—the feelings about being with her, not her."

What You Should Remember About Sex and Power

- Lovers are never absolutely equal.
- .Women obsess on withholding sex until the right moment, then give away their power in non-sexual ways. Most men wish they wouldn't. But, like anyone confronted with a doormat, they step on it.

- You may prefer having the slight power edge, or not having it. Don't let the "edge" consume more than 5 to 10 percent of the total space. Use of power is acceptable; abuse of power is not.
- Men under thirty may be more comfortable with women who have more power because their penises have not yet let them down in any significant way.

Part Three

AROUSAL

Lubricant Envy

••

Perhaps men are obsessed with reading our motives for wanting sex with them because they can never be as sure of our arousal as we are of theirs. An erection can't be faked. Ironically, the penis, the symbol of male power, makes men more vulnerable than women know. The penis lives outside the body, where it can always be observed. And intercourse depends so heavily on its enthusiastic participation. Yes, there can be desire in the absence of an erection—and an absence of desire in the presence of an erection. There can even be sex—wonderful, satisfying sex—in the absence of an erection. Yet few men greet its absence with a sanguine smile.

The erect penis symbolizes male arousal to us as well as to them. Years ago I read a section in Gail Sheehy's *Passages* in which a woman explained how to stuff a limp or partially erect penis into her vagina. Something bothered me about the description, but I didn't know what. Now I do. It was Sheehy's failure to mention there, or anywhere in her chapter on sex, that "stuffing" isn't necessary because good sex can take place without an erect penis. If she and the woman she quoted failed to grasp the fact then, can we blame men for having some problems with it now?

We say we don't want macho men—until we are confronted with a flaccid penis that "should" be quite hard. (This is the same penis that "shouldn't" be hard when we find its outstanding behavior embarrassing or offensive.) Then we smother it and him with encouragement and understanding. When that fails, we lay blame, at his side of the bed or ours.

Many women writers in the past decade have said or implied that a limp penis is man's way of putting the sexually aggressive woman in her place. They see erection as a power struggle he is determined to win, one way or another. Either he will persist when we don't want him or he will withhold when we do. Their assumptions are based on a belief that they would deny having: the machisma code, which holds that the penis can always be controlled by man or a sexually cunning and determined woman. If he and she can't, there's something wrong with him or her.

Were the penis not so visible, perhaps its arousal could be faked, as ours can. A dab of KY Jelly and a small bit of acting give us the prerogative of making love when our systems are not on full power. It's a nice privilege, one that allows us to dabble at lovemaking until our passions ignite, quickening the pace. He, on the other hand, is expected to start on high. Should she be in the mood before he is, she will focus her erotic energies on achieving his erection immediately. She will make love to the penis first, then the man. We, and they, continue to behave as though the myths were true, even in the face of daunting reality.

When recently asked to comment on how the sexual habits of Americans had changed since she wrote *Fear of Flying* in 1973, Erica Jong said, "There is more oral sex and more impotence." She is not the only one to notice. Several research studies have reported the same news. Sex therapists echo their findings with examples from their own caseloads.

We are told there is more oral sex because:

- Influenced by the sexual information explosion, we are now more apt to engage in the practice for fun.
- Aware of the female need for clitoral stimulation, we are now more likely to accept, even seek, separate orgasms, often achieved orally.
- Men can't perform adequately with women who are their sexual equals—and resort to oral sex to please them.

We are told there is more impotence because:
- The work ethic is killing the sex drive.
- Casual sex has deadened us to the thrill of intercourse.
- Men can't perform adequately with women who are their sexual equals.

We aren't told:

- Oral sex is the means by which men can feel sure they've "given" a woman an orgasm.
- The population is aging; and older males do not experience automatic erections whenever the thought of a female crosses their minds. The penis at twenty is fairly nondiscriminatory. The penis at thirty, forty, and beyond, is more selective.
- Woman's new freedom to seduce has led directly to men's new freedom *not* to be seduced. Of course, the penis was always erect when a woman met it fifty years ago. The man waited until it was to approach her.
- The inevitability of sex in relationships between men and women, married or not, has led to the inevitability of more situations in which the sex will not work, according to the code.

Sexual freedom has put more pressure on the man to perform and laid more emphasis on the penis than ever. Under the new machismo, giving her multiple orgasms is just as important as "scoring," or getting his, was under the old machismo. Imagine what it would be like if your vaginal secretions were monitored as closely as his erections are. KY Jelly would be sold under the counter, in natural woman scents.

6 The Enemies of Lust

···

"If a woman says, 'Come on, let's fuck,' I'm not interested—unless I know that fucking her doesn't necessarily mean I can own her. I can't explain it clearly. She has to have a built-in resistance. If she doesn't have that, then she'd better build resistance by withholding sex now and then. Without resistance, I can't stay aroused. That's what's wrong with marriage, especially marriage to the modern woman who thinks she has to be everything including an always available lover."

—John, age forty-five

The enemies of passion attack at the arousal level. Those enemies are exactly what women think they are: repetition of the same basic act, and age—aging bodies, the sagging jawlines and breasts of long-term wives or lovers, and even more importantly, aging relationships. Just as a man reaches the biological point where he needs more stimuli for arousal, he finds himself getting less from his long-term partner. Maybe he reaches for a new, if not younger, woman. Over the years, many men have written asking me variations of the same questions:

- How do I get my wife to participate in group sex or swapping?
- How do I get her to try something new (especially anal sex)?
- Though I love my wife, I'm having an affair (or I masturbate behind her back or fantasize wildly about other women) and I'm feeling guilty. Is my behavior normal?

Women, too, find intense passion can't be sustained without pause in long-term relationships. Desire waxes and wanes for both sexes. According to Princeton University demographic studies, which are backed by national and international research, the rate of intercourse declines rapidly after the first year of marriage (or togetherness). By the end of the second year, it is half the rate of the first year. More important than the age of the couple in determining frequency is the duration of the relationship. My own survey also proved that true: while less than a third of men say they are becoming more dependent on erotic stimuli, including sexy lingerie, dirty talk, and pornography, as *they* age, over half say they do become more dependent on such outside stimuli as a *relationship* ages.

Perhaps women, who are less excited by visual stimuli, become more dependent on romantic fantasy over time. It would be interesting to know if we do or not. Whatever the combination of motivating factors, we do know that women have more affairs than they once did. Kinsey found only 6 to 26 percent of the married women he studied strayed. Today's polls say up to 50 percent have done so. Men still have more adulterous affairs—up to 80 percent depending on the research source. They say they do it for the stimulation of variety, not from the need for romance. Some men believe we can better handle the boredom of sexual routine as long as we're feeling loved and/or having orgasms. We do become more easily aroused as we age than we did in our youth. And we are under far less pressure than men are to become aroused—and display that arousal.

Whether their answer is "swapping," or "cheating," or fantasizing, they ask:

How am I going to become aroused day after day with the same woman for the rest of my life?

"*Men respond to erotic comfort by developing an itch. We need that right combination of comfort and challenge. If a woman is always available to you, if she'll do anything you want her to do anytime, what's the difference in her and some sex-slave character from the works of de Sade?*" writes a thirty-year-old Texan.

The resistance factor again! The standard advice experts give women about putting the zing back into a marriage or keeping husbands at home, is to vary the sexual routine and/or give him what he wants in bed so he won't have to look in someone else's. Variety is always the spice of sexual life. But trying to give him everything he thinks he wants may be a bad idea, in addition to being impossible. (Isn't he really saying he wants less, not more?)

Every man sees himself in his sexual fantasies as getting more, and different, sex than he actually enjoys. But he is probably overcoming female resistance to get it—an important part of the scenario. His secret sexual self—determined in part by his personal interpretation of the code—is a man who fights erotic battles and wins them for everyone, pleasing him, pleasing her against her will. He is, of course, always aroused. It is harder for him to erect that fantasy around a compliant woman.

He also asks:

Why don't women understand that men can't help wanting to fuck every woman they see?

"It makes my woman mad when we are out together and I sneak glimpses of other women. She doesn't understand that a man's nature is not to be monogamous. I am making a sacrifice of my essential self to be true to her. When I get excited by other women, I make better love to her. Shouldn't she be glad of the results and not argue about how they're obtained?" writes a twenty-nine-year-old retail manager from the southwest.

Any man will, with varying rates of frequency, look at other women and imagine what it would be like to have sex with them. Men sexually objectify women, while women romanticize men. Men "look" at women as a collection of body parts, not people. When a man says his wandering eye doesn't mean he's unhappy with you, he's probably telling the truth. Former President Jimmy Carter dignified this male condition by labeling it "lusting in the heart." Apparently Rosalyn understood that looking, like jock talk, is meant to keep the penis encouraged.

Most men know they're only looking, but some men have convinced themselves they really do want to have sex with every woman they see. ("Even the ugly ones. All women have the same equipment, so in the dark, who cares if she's ugly?") Only social constraints and the bonds of love restrain their raging sex drive—or so they believe.

"Men have a sex drive. Women don't," one man explains. "The real truth about men is that we want to get laid as often as possible."

The man who accepts this philosophy is the "man's stud." He

has so internalized the macho code that he expresses not even a little niggling doubt when he answers yes to the question "Should a real man *always* want sex with an attractive woman?" He adheres as strictly to the old code as he does to the new: scoring counts as much as giving her multiple orgasms. He takes great pride in himself as an expert lover who knows exactly what a woman needs.

In some cases, the man's stud acts out his philosophy. Repeated conquests are necessary to maintaining his mental image of himself—and his state of sexual arousal. Women who love these men either reconcile themselves to male philandering or leave. (He is usually the man who would take his wife's adulterous behavior as a stake in the heart, because, for her, "it would mean something.")

"I hide my affairs from my wife, but I think she knows about them, or some of them, anyway," writes a thirty-seven-year-old lawyer. "I love my wife, but men are not naturally monogamous. One of my father's favorite stories is the one about President Coolidge and the rooster. Coolidge and his wife were being shown around a farm. Mrs. Coolidge inquired as to how one rooster was able to 'take care' of all those hens. When she was told he could have sex several times a day, she said, 'Tell that to Mr. Coolidge.' He asked if that was with the same hen or different hens. When told it was with different hens, he said, 'Tell that to Mrs. Coolidge.' You see my point. It's nature. Man is practically the only monogamous male in the animal kingdom. It isn't natural, but socially enforced."

Many male studs are monogamous husbands and lovers. They merely fantasize, leading a mental life as Don Juan. The secret self is as necessary to their arousal process as the philanderer's actual conquests are to his. While they may claim they are faithful "for her sake," they are probably happy for the excuse *not* to test their sexual mettle repeatedly with new women.

"If I could be happily married and have unlimited sex with other women, I would have it," says a thirty-two-year-old from Georgia. "I see beautiful women and I want to make love to them. But I can't act upon my desires. Men spend a lot of time being sexually frustrated. I find I can turn that frustration to my, and my wife's, advantage by bringing it home to her as lust. Does she need to know that what incites that lust isn't always her? No."

And still other men are talking about erotic change within the relationship—not multiple partners—when they talk about variety. They ask:

Why doesn't she understand that good sex is dependent on erotic change?

"My wife thinks love should be enough to arouse my passion. Ten years ago, it always was. Now it often isn't. She never refuses sex. She's always warm and loving and doesn't complain about the quality of our sex. But she does complain about the frequency. I want more, too, but I want her to be the woman of my fantasies, dressed in sexy, scanty costumes, behaving outrageously, wantonly, as if she lived for my cock alone," writes a husband of ten years.

It's unlikely he would be pleased if his wife suddenly turned into the wanton woman of his fantasies. Yes, he would like some erotic change—but not a total change. He's really saying: I want to be aroused as easily and often as I was ten years ago, but I'm not, which concerns me. While the man's stud assumes a new woman is the only cure, this man, the "woman's stud," believes in erotic change, or sexual variety, with the same woman. He does not accept that much of the time sex will be less than extraordinary. Often his woman shares his beliefs.

"When we were first living together five years ago, my girlfriend didn't want sex as often as I did," writes a twenty-seven-year-old man. "Now she wants it more. We fought then; we fight now. Part of it is we work different shifts. I used to get really excited when she woke me by taking my cock into my mouth. Now, sometimes, I think, I haven't got time for this now, or I'm too tired. Yet I think about other women a lot more than I did five years ago, too. It makes me feel guilty to fantasize about other women and masturbate while she's at work, then be too tired to satisfy her when she gets home."

What these men, and their women, share is the belief that any man should become aroused whenever she is available for sex. When time makes inroads on the arousal process, they blame themselves or each other for not introducing enough variety into their sex lives. Yes, variety is good, certainly much better than spending twenty years in the missionary position for ten minutes a night, two nights a week. But variety—like that other overworked word, communication—isn't a panacea for arousal anxiety.

"It's unrealistic to think a man will always be able to achieve full-strength arousal whenever his woman wants," writes a district sales manager from the northeast. "Sometimes sex can be something other than intercourse, like cuddling and masturbating her, or vice versa if he's the one with the hot drive and she's not. I would bet people deprive themselves of a lot of good physical contact because they think sex can only be the main act, fucking. And some men would take it further: sex can only be fucking when they feel strong enough to fuck her brains out. They don't feel like men unless their dicks are the consistency of iron rods. So a lot of nights a lot of people go to sleep feeling unloved, don't they?"

Other men also admit that part of the variety they desire in the sexual experience is occasional lovemaking at *less* than full thrust—or even occasional polite refusals.

"I'm on my second marriage," writes a Kentucky business owner. "My first wife did the total sexual-woman number when things settled down between us. At first it was exciting to come home to someone who might be lying naked on the floor with semisweet chocolate bits melting in her pussy. Then it got boring. Finally, it became—I hesitate to use this word because you'll think I'm the pussy—threatening. How much more did she want of me? Would I never be allowed a limp cock without an inferiority complex for having it?

"My second wife isn't always in the mood for sex. She can get every bit as hot as the first one did, but she has, thank God, her off days. You don't know how nice 'Not tonight, dear, I've got a headache' can sound sometimes."

And a doctor from Chicago says, "A man likes to think he's not getting as much as he could handle. He enjoys a low level of sexual frustration, especially as he gets older. The main motor of his sex drive runs off resistance. Women don't like to hear this, but he doesn't want what he can get too easily. He particularly doesn't want to wonder if he's going to be able to keep up the pace or let her down."

All this talk of resistance makes it sound as if men want an erotic battle every night. Not true. But the suspicion it might be is what leads many female advice givers to warn, "Play hard to get." What men want is a lover's acceptance of their sexuality, at its highs and lows. They already labor under their own myth. They can read her determination to arouse them when they aren't aroused—or her near-complete submission to them, sexually and otherwise—as manifestations of her own myth. She is expecting them always to be ready, to please her totally, to assume responsibility for her. They are understandably scared.

The "resistance" they want is not a manufactured one. The woman who plays hard to get can't hide her neediness if it's there. Repeatedly, men tell me they want an intelligent woman, not a "bimbo" or "consummate game player" or "someone who is willing to turn into another person for the sake of pleasing her man." Intelligent, *independent* women have a natural resistance men find sexy and appealing. ("A dumb woman may be okay for a blow job," explains a twenty-nine-year-old Texan, "but not for real sex. You need something other than a body to fasten on to when you're making love.") True resistance comes from a partner who:

● Knows and accepts her sexual needs and desires, as she does his.
● Doesn't expect him to *always* fulfill those needs for her as she knows she can't *always* fulfill his.
● And won't give up *all* of herself because they are lovers.

"Women have a stupid side," John says. "When they placate their man—in and out of bed—at the expense of being their own person, they're being saps. They're also taking something away from him. They're making it too easy for him. They're taking away his challenge, making it too easy for him to get fat, lazy, complacent.

Sure, he'll push for everything, total control. That doesn't mean he wants it when he gets it."

He almost certainly doesn't.

What You Should Remember About Male Arousal

- Because he responds more strongly to visual stimuli than you do, he will be aroused by the sight of an attractive woman while you may only admire an attractive male.
- Even if he wants to believe he could, or should, be able to act upon that arousal, he probably won't.
- If you no longer arouse him as easily or as often as you did, don't treat the situation as a problem that can be automatically solved by giving him more of whatever it is you know, or think, he likes. Don't try so hard. Accept the natural ebb and flow of desire.
- Sexual variety is wonderful. But one of the variations you should consider is nonpressured, non-goal-oriented affection. Hold him in your arms and stroke his hair. Don't make him feel it has to lead somewhere.

7 The Friendly Beaver

••

"If it's meant to excite a woman, it's erotica. If it's meant to excite a man, it's pornography. Come on, is that fair?"

—James, an erotic writer

Fair, no. But, true. If you doubt it, check out the erotica on sale at your neighborhood gay and lesbian bookstore. Andrea Dworkin, the radical-feminist crusader against pornography, is also the author of torrid lesbian prose that often ventures into S&M territory. (No, I can't explain to you why it is acceptable for a woman to hurt another woman while it is not acceptable for a man to hurt a woman. Presumably she can.)

Since Hugh Hefner launched *Playboy* at the kitchen table of his suburban Chicago home in 1954, publications and videos aimed at arousing men have been attacked by women, preachers like Jim Bakker, and "concerned citizens." (Child pornography and snuff films, illegal and morally indefensible, are not part of the mainstream porn discussed in this book. Nor is extremely violent sadomasochistic material.) On the other hand, collections of erotica by women, such as Lonnie Barbach's *Pleasures* and *Erotic Interludes* and *Deep Down: The New Sensual Writing by Women*, edited by Laura Chester, have been widely praised. One difference is that women's sexually explicit material is nearly always verbal, seldom accompanied by pictures.

Most men are turned on by pornographic literature and books— and by X-rated videos. Over 90 percent of the men in my survey cited one or both categories as turn-ons. The majority use the materials as erotic aides, the jump starters for masturbatory or other sexual experiences. (We are not talking about that small percentage of men who obsess on pornography—for example, spending hours alone with their collections and preferring their masturbatory experiences to sex with real women.) Shere Hite, in *The Hite Report on Male Sexuality*, found the overwhelming majority of men preferred the high-quality artfully posed nude photos in *Penthouse* and *Playboy* to the explicit sex depicted in the more cheaply produced publications.

Lonnie Barbach says, "For most men, looking at *Playboy, Penthouse*, or *Forum* is a form of arousal; the man isn't looking for another woman or comparing his partner to the woman on the page. He does it because it's fun. He doesn't see it as degrading. Men use visual stimulation as a turn-on, women don't. They respond to physical touching and emotional interaction."

The question men have most often asked me about porn is:

How do I get her to share pornographic books, magazines, or videos with me?

"I think it would inspire her to try something new. She's not into anything different, even the wearing of sexy lingerie. She says the magazines I like are either 'sick' or 'dirty.' She says they exploit women. I say the pictures are a turn-on; and the stories are about great sex, for both men and women. What's wrong with that?"

Obviously I don't think there's anything wrong with the magazines this man likes. They provide men with solid information about sex techniques and the sexual needs of women, the same kind of information we get from our magazines, only written in their language. They give him a safe outlet for his fantasies. And far more often than you realize if you aren't a regular reader, they feature stories and letters about women who take the sexual initiative.

Women who find these magazines offensive say they objectify women, which they find distasteful. Porn does objectify women, because it is designed to arouse men, and men sexually objectify women. They do so because they are able to separate love and sex. Most women can't, either because we are made differently or socially brainwashed into believing we are. Whether you find that palatable or not doesn't change reality. Your attitude may force your man to swear he *never* thinks of a woman as a collection of erotic parts, but he's lying to you, and maybe himself.

"A man will tell you if he's a breast man, a leg man, an ass lover," says James. "While a woman might admire the passing male buttocks, she will never describe herself as a butt lover. Even the most physical-parts-conscious woman won't fixate and fantasize on those parts. When she fantasizes making love to a man, she is caught up in a whole-body, total-emotions experience. A man, however, will see those spectacular tits walking past him and imagine himself jerking off between them. That's just how he is."

A man's ability to objectify a woman in the physical sense sets him apart from us. We, however, objectify him in a different way, as a success object. Many women who find pornography offensive fail to see how a man could be offended by our books and magazines, which far too often treat him as an asset we can purchase with our charm, cunning, and beauty. Because sex is equated with sin in our puritanical society while female financial dependence is linked with God and apple pie, these women are able to feel comfortable in their position. They use pornography as another proof that men are a lower species. Some men are beginning to realize an object is an object, its packaging notwithstanding.

"My ex-wife was holier than thou about porn," writes a steamfitter from the Midwest. "She made me feel guilty for buying *Penthouse* and *Playboy* every month. She said I was sick and immature because I needed more than true love to become aroused. Then I got laid off for six months. She had to get a job to supplement my unemployment. She was angry at me for letting her down, scared I'd never find another job . . . things were awful between us until I got into work again. She never wanted sex. I learned something from the experience. My paycheck turned her on more than photos of nude women turn me on."

Even women who tolerate their husbands' reading habits claim they aren't turned on by pornography themselves. Research studies have shown that women, like men, *do* respond physically to pornographic words and images. We experience elevated heartbeats, increased vaginal secretions—all the usual signs of arousal. The women tested claimed they were not aroused, though evidence indicated they were. Apparently they were able to hide their arousal from themselves because they have been taught to believe porn is morally offensive, especially to women. But many men would like to share this particular arousal experience with their women.

"I got my wife to read *Penthouse Letters* with me, and now she's likely to be the one who brings it home," says a fan. "We read the letters and stories out loud to each other, which makes us both hot. Sometimes we try the things in the letters. Or they inspire us to try something similar. It spices up our sex life."

The second question men frequently ask about porn is:

Why is she so threatened by X-rated movies?

"I love my wife's body. She has fantastic breasts. I love to shoot my hot come all over them. She says this is an idea I got from the videos, which makes her nervous. The whole concept makes her nervous, because she says she can't compare to the women in them. I don't have a mega-cock either, but I get off on watching one pump. Why is she so hung up about her body?"

He probably did "get the idea" from videos that ejaculating outside his partner's body was a mutually erotic experience. My increased mail on this sex practice definitely coincided with the surge in video sales. Many men asked why their own measure of semen was less than what they saw splashed on the screen. (Answer: The movies supplement the real thing with fake "come.")

Most don't get inferiority complexes from watching videos (though a few men are threatened a bit by the penis size of some of the male stars). They don't understand our self-consciousness about our nude bodies in comparison to the glossy ones on screen—any more than we understand their concern about penis size. We fear they're comparing our bodies to those of porn stars and finding us lacking. In fact, some women believe men want to watch the videos rather than look at the real woman beside them. That isn't true.

Men are not as hard on us as we are on ourselves. While they might say they want slim women, their definition of slim isn't as exacting as ours. They are fairly forgiving of excess curves on their women, and they tend to focus on (or objectify) her best body parts. Most men like the Fifties ideal, as personified by Marilyn Monroe, a body type now considered "fat" by the arbiters of style and beauty.

The wife who has "fantastic breasts" may be frankly fat by the standards of her peers.

Men treat the X-rated video as a sex aide. Men feel the films are best enjoyed with a female partner. Like her, a man would be bored after the first fifteen minutes, too, if he did nothing but watch. This is participatory erotica.

"I am old enough to remember when guys showed stag films out in the garage," says a Virginian. "They were of poor quality, grainy, badly shot, no sound. Not even very titillating. We watched them because it was something guys were supposed to do together, like smoke cigars, play poker, and get drunk. Things have changed for the better. Videos are meant to be shown on the bedroom TV, where they can really do some good in the world."

And a man from South Dakota says, "My wife is usually the one who rents the videos because she works in a mall that has a video rental store. About once a week she brings home something hot for the two of us to enjoy together. We got into mutual masturbation as a form of foreplay through videos. She gets off on watching me come. We do more oral sex now. I'd say our sex life has improved quite a bit."

Whether pornography encourages people to experiment or sparks their passion or merely feeds their fantasies, it has become increasingly a sexual tool for couples. Much has been made in recent years of the growing violent content of some forms of pornography. The less-discussed new trend is couples-oriented videos featuring romantic story lines, softer photography, and romantic music. Many are produced and directed by women, most notably former porn star Candida Royalle, owner of Femme Productions. If you have been refusing your man's suggestion of bedroom erotica, rent one of Royalle's films. You might change your mind about porn.

Why You Shouldn't Make an Issue of Mainstream Porn

- His need for other erotic stimuli does not reflect negatively on your sex appeal.

- He does not expect you to look, or behave, like the woman on screen.
- You can benefit from the knowledge of sex techniques he gains from porn and from his heightened sense of arousal.
- He doesn't censor your reading material, does he?

8 Maybe You'd Rather Not Know

....

"For a period of time following my divorce I had violent fantasies about my ex-wife. I had her bound and gagged, suspended from a large gold hook in the ceiling. I kept her hanging until her body was covered with sweat and trembling from muscle spasms. Tears were running down her face, and she was moaning behind the gag. Then I whipped her, all over her body, from the neck to the knees. My prick swelled to twice its normal size. Sometimes I raped her from a standing position. Sometimes I untied her, threw her to the floor, and raped her anally. When it was over, she admitted nobody had ever given it to her as good as I had. It was therapeutic."

—A forty-two-year-old Midwestern corporate executive

This man has never had a real-life S&M experience. Nor, he says, does he want one. Nor was he ever violent toward his ex-wife. The divorce is two years into his past, and he is involved with another woman, whom he loves. He still has fantasies, even the occasional violent one, but none about his ex. Most men do fantasize. Their fantasies may include some violence, usually in the form of light spanking or whipping requested or desired by the woman who needs it to bring her to orgasm, or violence administered to him by a woman, for much the same reason: the granting of permission to feel.

The average man has eight sexual fantasies per hour, ranging from his fleeting erotic appreciation of a passing pair of legs to mental images of penetration. Like us, he uses fantasy to stimulate arousal for masturbation or intercourse. His fantasies fall roughly into the same general categories as ours do:

- Replacement of a regular partner with a real or imagined one.
- Sex with more than one partner.
- Homosexual sex.
- Forced sex.
- Exhibitionist sex.
- And one category that is distinctly male: anal sex.

As Nancy Friday discovered while researching *Men in Love*, the ultimate collection of male fantasies, his sexual daydreaming tends to be more violent and far less personal than ours. Inspired by a man we've met or seen, we create romantic stories including an introduction and seduction, then ultimately sex. This man is given romantic qualities far in excess of those he actually possesses. Sometimes our sex fantasies may run like a Hollywood love story from the Fifties, culminating neither in intercourse nor orgasm. Even in the privacy of our minds, we seldom have anonymous sex or sex purely for the sake of physical release.

The favorite female fantasy is one of rape/force, or as Friday labels it, the "he made me do it!" scenario. Of course, in reality, women do not want to be raped. The fantasy merely signifies our need for permission to enjoy sex, which we get by daydreaming about a swashbuckling hero who takes us against our will, thus freeing us sexually. Naturally one would expect men to have the corresponding fantasy of being the romantic rapist who conquers us.

Friday was surprised to discover "*One of the major themes in male fantasy is the abdication of activity in favor of passivity.* . . . It turns out that men's favorite fantasies are not about raping/forcing/making women do it. In fantasy, men want exactly what women want: to be done to.*"

Like us, many men need permission to enjoy sex. Their fantasies of being overcome by a voracious woman or being erotically punished give them the excuse to let go. The mental whip takes away his guilt, too. If we could see the film running through a man's mind, however, we might be so embarrassed, appalled, or frightened by its content, we wouldn't analyze its meaning or compare it to our own. Sometimes he is also worried and confused about what goes on inside his head. The question men most frequently asked about their fantasies is:

Am I abnormal?

"In my fantasies I am often having sex with a woman and another man. She sucks me while masturbating him with her hand. When we shift positions, I suck her fingers while she blows him, and he jerks me off. The taste of him on her hand excites me. He and I are both hard again, and she is begging us to satisfy her. She lowers herself onto my cock and he enters her asshole from behind. I can feel his cock through her thin membrane. It's like I'm fucking both of them, and it's the most exciting thing I've ever done. We all come at the same time. I'm not gay or bisexual. Is it abnormal to have these fantasies?" writes a Cleveland tax accountant.

Men are frequently concerned about their homosexual or violent fantasies, but these fantasies are, according to the experts, *normal*, unless they become obsessive. There is not a great body of psychological literature dealing with sexual fantasies, which is surprising considering their prevalence and importance in our lives. Before Nancy Friday, no one had extensively cataloged the experience, and not even the great C. G. Jung had much to say about the subject. Therapists generally believe it is the frequency of the troubling fantasies rather than their content that indicates a potential problem.

Thinking something doesn't necessarily mean one has done, is doing, or will do it. In my own survey fewer than one-fifth of the respondents reported a homosexual experience, and almost half of those men who did claimed they were isolated incidents that had taken place largely in their youth. (I heard from only a handful of bisexual men, lending further support to a theory shared by readers of the mail sent to sex magazines: Bisexuality is more common among women than men.) Yet more than half the total surveyed had the occasional homosexual fantasy.

Rape and/or bondage and S&M fantasies were even more common. Participation in bondage is less so (35 percent, mostly once or twice, from curiosity) and S&M (less than 30 percent) even less common. In her study of male masochists, Friday reported the ratio of masochists to sadists as four to one. My survey and the letters I've received at the magazines reinforce her findings.

According to Friday, "Underneath the sadistic facade the fantasy has a contradictory story to tell: The man seems to be saying that he inflicts his will on the victim not to be cruel, but to force the inhibited woman into pleasure she could not accept in any other way. [He] hurts his sexual partner 'just enough to give pleasure.' "

The S&M fantasies, as Friday has noted, also express man's deep ambivalence about women. On the one hand, they lust after us; on the other, they are angry at the power we hold over them. The masochist fantasy, she believes, "illustrates an inversion of anger . . . born of the same rage . . . as the sadist's."

Again, the daydreams shouldn't be confused with reality.

A northeastern professor writes: "In my fantasies, there is no violence in the sense of inflicting physical pain, hitting anyone (I am vehemently opposed to physical abuse of any woman by anyone) etc. However, I am very aroused by imagining a pretty, deliciously dressed woman being bound and gagged, rendered submissive, and slowly undressed and enjoyed in every way possible by her captor/ sex-starved slavemaster.

"I am well aware that such fantasies, making women I lust after into my sex slaves, are objectively degrading to women. However, I also believe these fantasies may derive from my sometimes enormous sense of frustration and resentment at the power women exert, through the use of sex, over me and other men."

And a man on the other side of the mental whip explains both his fantasy and his shame: "I imagine a tall strong woman built like Brigitte Nielsen dressed in black leather bikini and high-heeled boots that reach to her thighs. She has a cat-o'-nine-tails in one hand. She slaps it lightly against her boot as I undress and kneel before her. Naked, I lean forward to kiss her feet. She brings the whip down across my buttocks, and my prick gets hard. Again and again she brings the whip down. I think I won't be able to handle any more and suddenly she is finished with the whip. She straps an enormous dildo on her and fucks me up the ass. I feel like I am being ripped open. The pain moves through my balls like waves. I come hard.

"I would die of shame if my wife could read my mind. We have a normal sex life. I don't know what these thoughts mean, maybe I am sick."

In spite of their concerns about them, men do ask me if they should share these and particularly other, less-threatening fantasies with their wives or lovers. Many believe sharing does, or should, lead to acting out. The second most asked question about sexual fantasies is:

How do I get her to act it out?

"*I have fantasies of having sex with my wife and her best friend. In my favorite one, I come home unexpectedly in the middle of the day and find them in bed together. They are going at it hard, mouths to cunts, panting and moaning, so they aren't aware I'm in the room. My cock gets hard. I unbuckle my belt in preparation to pulling off my pants. Then I decide to bring the belt down across my wife's sweet little ass, which is wiggling attractively in the air. She gasps and collapses on top of her friend. They look at me and blush, but it's clear they can't stop now. I throw my clothes off and jump in bed between them. Eagerly they both turn to me. My wife wants to ride my cock, but I tell her, 'Company first.' Her friend climbs on while my wife straddles my face. I tongue her furiously, bringing her to explosive orgasm as her friend is writhing in ecstasy on top of me. The afternoon is an erotic heaven with me having both women orally, anally, and otherwise. So how do I get my wife to try a threesome for real? Should I share my fantasy with her?*" writes a reader.

His first question is but another variation on the common theme: How do I get my partner to give me what I want sexually? My answer is: Introduce your desire as a subject rather than a request. If possible, find an erotic passage in a book or film that expresses what you would like to do. Read or show it to her. See how much interest she has in the subject before you ask. Then, ask nicely.

The above reader's second question isn't an easy one. I have never given an unequivocal answer to that or any query requiring a judgment rooted in psychological knowledge rather than well-documented facts, or to a query requiring more than a simple opinion born of common sense and good sexual manners. The experts, who often don't agree, advise sharing fantasies with caution only, no matter how well you know and trust your partner.

"Perhaps the greatest misconception about sexual fantasies is that they are suppressed wishes," says Friday.

Believing this, some men guiltily shelter their private fantasies, while others seek to share them for the purpose of making them real. (Still others keep their fantasies private, without the guilt, using them when necessary as arousal aides.) Judging from my mail, the sharers are selective. They choose to share those fantasies that are likely to be acceptable in theory, if not in practice; for example, sex with another partner or two women, anal sex, bondage, sex in exotic settings or public places, even light S&M scenes. They are less likely to disclose homosexual or heavily violent fantasies.

Telling doesn't necessarily lead to action, and when it does, the action may be disappointing, or even rob the fantasy of its future power to excite.

"Talking about some of my fantasies to the women I've known has gotten them more excited," writes a southeastern business manager in his early thirties. "I date women of all ages, and the older ones are less threatened by hearing I dream about being held captive by a group of sexually voracious Amazons who force me to satisfy the whole tribe daily. Younger women get their feelings hurt hearing you'd even think of fucking anyone else.

"When you move beyond talking to the next level, of participating, it gets weirdly disappointing. For instance, I convinced a woman to act out one of my favorite fantasies, of picking up a high-class call girl in a hotel bar. She dressed the part, including no underwear, and acted it beautifully. Taking her out of that bar was a hot trip. Back home, the sex was sex. Nothing different. But she wanted to act like a hooker again the following week. I saw it as too much trouble to go to just for a fuck, and I was sorry I'd brought the whole idea up. I couldn't tell her that, of course. I would have looked stupid."

Another man in his thirties writes: "Talking about my fantasies killed them for me. I had all these elaborate sexual stage sets in my head and I had to trash them and build new ones because pulling them out into the light destroyed them. No, she wasn't critical of them. It wasn't her fault. They just aren't meant to live in the light."

For many men, some fantasies are an expression of the taboo. If you can share the taboo, even act it out, then it's no longer forbidden. No longer a thrilling dirty secret, the fantasy loses its power to arouse them automatically. In other cases, acting out doesn't rob the fantasy of its mental appeal, but it doesn't exactly work in the flesh as planned in the brain either.

"My girlfriend and I had talked at length about our mutual bondage-and-anal-rape fantasies," says a Connecticut professional. "We agreed to try one. First, I stripped her, tied her wrists together behind her back, and put her over my lap for a spanking. I started with light blows and gradually delivered harder ones, stopping periodically to play with her clit. She was getting so hot at one point I was afraid she'd come too soon. We had agreed to tease her sexually and thus prolong the game as long as possible before relieving her. I started spanking her again. She was jerking in my lap, trying to pull away from my hand when all that motion coupled with the sight of her rosy wiggling ass made me shoot my wad too soon.

"I was surprised at how powerfully I had reacted to spanking her. If she had told me to untie her and halt the game then, I would have. But she was still hot as blazes. She said, 'Don't quit on me now.' I assumed she meant keep playing the game. I told her she'd have to get me hard again first. So I made her kneel in front of me, sucking my cock while I twisted her nipples in my fingers. When I was big and hard inside her mouth, she pulled back and said, 'Now do me.'

"I took that to mean we were taking the scene from the top again. I threw her over my lap and began slamming my hand against her butt. She protested loudly. I thought it was part of the game and shoved her panties into her mouth as a gag. My hand was stinging. I took my belt and gave her a dozen or so good strokes. She was jerking around in my lap so vigorously I was afraid I'd come again. I put her facedown on the bed, hands still tied behind her back,

with her legs drawn up beneath her, tush sticking up and out—
the point being she couldn't press her clit down against the mattress
and bring herself off. I took out the gag. She was gasping and
crying, 'You hurt me.'

"I buried my face in her burning ass and began licking her asshole
and diddling her pussy, which was swollen and clotted with secretions. She begged me to fuck her. I did, in the ass, as we'd planned,
but I was too rough, and in that position she couldn't get any
traction on her clit. I came again, but it was a little disappointing
because in our fantasy she was supposed to have the orgasm of her
life now. By this time she was sobbing almost hysterically. I finally
caught on that she'd wanted to end the game sometime back and
just get fucked. When she calmed down, she did let me bring her
to orgasm orally. But we weren't comfortable with each other for a
long time afterward. We were both frightened of the powerful
passions we'd unleashed."

Fantasies of bondage, anal sex, and S&M obviously should only
be acted out with the greatest care. (Another fantasy with a hidden
ensnaring web beneath the surface: man being overcome by sexually
voracious woman who uses him until he, and she, collapse. In real
life, the woman who can't be sated represents one of his greatest
sexual fears.) Some men have brought such fantasies, both theirs
and their woman's, to life successfully. The secret, they say, is scaling
down the activity from the level on which it is imagined. Or, as
one man says, "Slap lightly, but think heavy thoughts. You still
have to keep a good part of it up in your brain."

What You Should Understand About Fantasies

- They are, for the most part, not wishes. With some exceptions,
  their power to excite depends on their never being enacted.
- His aren't as pretty as yours.
- They are only a problem if he becomes obsessed with them. (Choco-
  olate, if you become obsessed with it, can become a problem.)
- They are an arousal tool in his erotic kit. Don't look for too many
  hidden meanings.

9 Selective Arousal

● ●

"I only enjoy sex with extremely attractive women. They must be very fit, otherwise I have difficulty in getting aroused. I particularly like younger women and have only had relationships with women twenty to twenty-five years younger than myself in the past ten years. I am currently fifty-three. My ideal is mid- to late twenties, provided she is very fit and very attractive."
       —A corporate vice-president from the northeast

This man's qualifications for a lover read like Hugh Hefner's personal arousal criteria. Women over thirty both dread falling for him and assume he is far more typical of men than he really is. He may be the most frustrating, disappointing, even hurtful man you'll ever meet—if you're foolish enough to think you can change him. Though he may feel a little guilty or embarrassed about his limitations, he is unlikely to change without therapy—which he is unlikely to get as long as beautiful young women are attracted to older, wealthier, more powerful men.

The selective arousal categories are: hair color, body size and/or type, and age. They represent the only socially acceptable fetishes. It isn't okay to worship a foot; it is okay to worship a breast. There are some few men who will never want anyone but a blonde, or a thin woman, or a twenty-five-year-old. They can't help it. As the above writer explains: he has difficulty becoming erect with any other type.

If you aren't the type, you will have to change what can be changed. (Is this man worth it when there are so many other men who would love you the way you are?) Otherwise, forget him.

Men who fall in love with hair color often ask:

How many other men only get it up for blondes?

"I am twenty-nine and have never had a woman who wasn't blond. I

prefer natural, but they are fairly scarce. I don't mind a good bleach job. Often you can't tell the difference. But why don't women who bleach their heads do their pubes? Real dark pubic hairs can be distracting," writes a golf pro.

Some women actually do bleach their pubic hair to match their heads. Blond is still the number-one hair-color choice among white men who have a *strong* preference—a group representing not more than 10 percent of my mail. According to photographers specializing in centerfold spreads, brunettes have gained strength in recent years. Redheads get both strong pro and con reactions. Men love them or hate them. Black men seem to like red hair as much as blond on white women. Whatever a man prefers, his choice is probably tied to early erotic experiences, good or bad.

"My first lover was a blonde," says a thirty-year-old. "She was wonderful. I was sold on blondes. Whenever I see a blond head that looks like hers, my cock does a little wave."

A thirty-nine-year-old Minnesota cop thinks his blonde fixation started in puberty: "I began masturbating to the nudes in *Penthouse* and *Playboy*. Back in those days, they were more often than not blondes, all-American-girl types with big breasts. When I was old enough to get laid for real, I sought out blondes who looked, at least in my imagination, as much as possible like those pinups. Come to think of it, the only resemblance most of the real girls had to the women in magazines was that hair. So I guess I focused on the hair to get turned on and my mind filled in the remembered details."

A fifty-year-old New York editor who eschews blondes in favor of tall sturdy brunettes explains his preference: "I keep trying to find my first wife all over again. She left me for another man six years ago. I haven't dated anyone but a tall brunette since."

And some men only like women of a certain color.

"I am white," writes a twenty-nine-year-old, "but I am only attracted to Hispanic or light black-skinned women. I have never had sex with a woman of my own race."

Those who choose body type and/or size ask:

Why can't I get excited by a woman who doesn't have big tits?

"I am very fond of a woman friend and would like to get romantically involved with her. She wants me. It would be great—a woman I could love, like, and respect. But she has no chest. We've had sex once. It wasn't great. I had to fantasize her body different to enjoy it. Should I just keep doing that or give up on the idea of being with her or ask her to get breast-enlargement surgery?" writes a *"Southern gentleman."*

Several men have written to ask for suggestions on how to convince women to have breast-augmentation surgery performed. My first thought was, How shallow of them. But my second thought was, They are no more shallow than the thousands of women who do have the surgery done each year simply because they've always wanted to have bigger breasts. Ours is not a society in which female body acceptance flourishes. Our willingness to change ourselves cosmetically or surgically hasn't gone unnoticed by men. We should expect some of them to develop the same mind-set about our bodies that we have: It can be changed.

Breasts, legs, and buttocks are the body parts upon which men tend to focus. Most *prefer* a certain type, determined in part by their racial, ethnic, and cultural backgrounds. Some few *require* it for arousal. A man's specific type may be defined by breast size or the length and quality of her legs, or the size of her whole body. Some men only like small breasts. Others choose lean or fat women.

"My wife is fifty, maybe sixty pounds overweight," writes a Chicago bus driver, "which is exactly the way I like her. I want something to grab on to when I'm riding her. I like the look and feel of her flesh, the soft rolls of her belly rippling as she steps out of her clothes. Skinny women leave me cold. You could put me naked in bed with one, and I swear my prick would lie there and go to sleep."

Monroe, a black writer who lives in New Orleans, says, "The closer a man is to the poor side of his racial group, the fatter he likes his woman. It means she's healthy, and he can afford to feed her. White men whose roots go back a ways like their women skinny.

But look at the white Polish immigrant in Chicago or the Puerto Rican in the Bronx or the black laborer in Mississippi. He wants flesh, erotic security. Thin bodies, man, they leave him drooping in his pants."

Monroe, however, has "overcome" his "racial training." He likes, he says, "All types, colors, sizes, as long as they're smart and sassy and over twenty-one. The only thing that turns me off is a bimbo. I panic. I think, Does she expect me to do this all by myself?"

Men who are not aroused by women of a certain age ask:

Why am I not aroused by women over thirty or thirty-five?

"As soon as they begin to show signs of aging, I can't perform with them. There is something about wrinkled, pocked, and pitted flesh which renders it untouchable. I am an educated, intelligent man, but I can't overcome my aversion to aging female flesh. Men do not look like this as we age. I am in love with a beautiful young woman and would like to marry her, but this is holding me back. Will I fall out of love with her as she ages? Is it a common erotic dread?" writes a forty-nine-year-old manufacturer from the southwest.

Fortunately for us, it is not *that* common an "erotic dread." While most men are attracted to firm young bodies, few are exclusively excited to arousal by them. (To balance the equation, some young men prefer the older woman as sex partner.) Psychiatric professionals tell us man's fear of sex with an older woman is nothing but a manifestation of his own fears about aging and dying. When the fear becomes extremely pronounced, it renders him impotent with any but the youngest, firmest maiden.

"I feel young again with a woman half my age," a fifty-five-year-old contractor admits. "My cock sings. That's what it's all about, isn't it? At this point in life, you have to choose between the cock and doing the right thing by a woman you've been with a good number of years. Whatever you choose, you can't make the cock choose different. You either go with him or do without him."

Obviously there is nothing a woman his age can do to change this man's mind. He has linked sex with female youthfulness deep within the part of his brain that controls arousal. If *he* wanted to change, he surely could with the help of a therapist. But he doesn't.

Another motive attributed to the age-selective man is insecurity. He chooses, or so the logic goes, a younger woman who has less experience than he because he shrinks from sexual comparison with other men. And he expects her to be less demanding as well as less knowledgeable. While this may be true of some age fetishists, they don't talk about it. Maybe they fail to recognize that sexual insecurity within themselves.

A sixty-year-old entrepreneur says, "It doesn't matter why I am only turned on by young and beautiful women. I can afford them. That's what matters. Does anybody ask why I'm only turned on by a Mercedes and not a Ford? Of course not. It would be silly to question a rich man's taste in cars, wouldn't it?"

He doesn't sound insecure, but he doesn't sound like anyone I regret not knowing (in the biblical sense) either.

The Salient Fact About Selective Arousal

- Understanding why his arousal is tied to limited physical requirements may make you feel better . . . but the knowledge won't change him.

10 Why He Asks You to Do *That*

••

"I want my wife to shave her pussy, and she's reluctant to do it. I am really turned on by the sight of a smooth-shaven pussy. I fantasize her like that, with dewdrops of lust clinging to her sex."

—A new husband

Her idea of sexual variety is likely to be a different position, a night at an expensive hotel, or an orgasm obtained through oral sex. Most of her suggestions for rekindling desire in a cooled-down relationship are romantic ones that have more to do with setting than sexual technique. More comfortable with sexual routine than he, she desires ambience. Her greater need is erotic security so her sexuality can blossom. His is erotic variety. He wants something other than a dozen roses and a love note on the pillow.

As a columnist, I received hundreds of letters from men asking why wives or girlfriends wouldn't shave off their pubic hair; talk dirty in bed; make love in garter belt, black stockings, and high, high heels; masturbate for them; or allow them to sniff their underarms and crotches as part of foreplay. Many men wanted their women to make love in public places or go out for the evening without underwear beneath their skimpy clothing. The men in my survey harbored the same desires. Almost 90 percent of them rated more than one of these a turn-on, and several wrote explaining why they craved stimuli women didn't.

"When I was seventeen, the mere sight of a partially clad or naked woman was almost enough to cause me to have an orgasm," writes a thirty-eight-year-old technical services director. "As the years went by, the edge came off my sex drive. It takes more than just nudity to arouse me now. I was married for five years, and the beginning sex was great, but we kept doing the same things over and over. I did my best to try to introduce her to variety, but she wouldn't do anything different.

"Now I can be aroused fairly easy in a new relationship, but as time goes by with the same woman, I need stronger visual cues. She has to jolt me, give me erotic shocks to the penis, by showing me something I didn't expect to see—her pussy shaved, or a bra with the nipples cut out. She has to do more to turn me on."

Many women find these requests threatening. They bring us face-to-face with a darker side of male sexuality than we want to see. And they make us feel unappealing. According to our logic, he shouldn't need more than our warm, loving bodies in a new negligee; and if he does, there's something wrong with one of us. We don't understand how much his sexual arousal is dependent on visual excitement. The new is exciting. The familiar, repeated over and over again, is less so. That has nothing to do with love.

What men most often ask about variety is:

How do I get her to shave her pubis?

"I love the look of a shaved pubis. I also love the feel. There is nothing quite like fucking a woman who has no pubic hair. No resistance at the groin level. She seems so vulnerable. When she's hot, the beads of moisture show around the edges of her sex lips. Why don't more women do this when it's so sexy?" writes a northwestern printer.

I would guess most women find it difficult enough keeping the hair growth off their legs and underarms. Who has time for this, too? Besides, the hair is extremely itchy in the early regrowth stage, and some women find shaving irritates the sensitive skin. More important, women fear that a man who wants his wife to shave her pubis is really expressing lust for prepubescent girls.

"I don't believe this is true at all," writes a California psychologist who participated in my survey. "This is not one of my particular turn-ons, so I feel safe from the conflict-of-interest charge in defending it. The shaved look appeals to some men some of the time because it makes a woman appear vulnerable. If she's a powerful woman or he's feeling like a weak man at the moment, it can be a very sexy look. It evens the odds. We're always physically vulnerable. We have it all hanging out all the time."

The shaved look is popular with S&M devotees. (De Sade's literary women were clean-shaven.) As an occasional erotic jolt, it also works for men who are not interested in S&M or young girls. And, it probably works best, as one man says, "in small doses. If a woman shaves once or twice a year, that's hot. If she did it all the time, it would get boring."

And then men ask:

Why won't she talk dirty for me in bed?

"My woman is a sophisticated and successful mortgage banker, the proverbial 'wouldn't say shit if she had a mouthful' lady. When she says, 'Fuck me, suck me, ram your rod in my slit,' it drives me wild. But I have to beg her to do it. Why is she so opposed?" writes a twenty-nine-year-old lawyer.

Many men find dirty talk an erotic stimulus, but only if the conversation is private. He isn't looking for a woman who can verbally hold her own with a marine at a bar. No, he wants a woman to say those nasty words only for him.

"Part of the thrill," admits a fifty-one-year-old New Yorker, "is realizing she'd never talk that way for anybody else. It's like seeing her naked, only better. A naked body isn't as personal."

Another man adds, "I like fuck talk, but I want to be the one who asks for it. If she starts spouting blue words without persuasion, I know she's done it before for some other man. It's his little trick he taught her."

And surprisingly, many men want her to keep some clothes on. They ask:

Is it crazy to want her to leave something on?

"There's so much nudity in our world that I find a bit of clothing a bigger turn-on now. It drives me wild when a woman makes love in a teddy or garter belt and stockings as a change of pace. The feel of the nylon on my skin when she wraps her legs around me is electric," writes a lab technician.

I particularly remember the first letter I received from a man who wanted his wife to keep her high heels on while they had sex. In my mind, I could see her trying to make love without digging her heels into his back. Maybe an occasional spike would have added to his pleasure. On the other hand, he might have enjoyed taking them off her feet when they got in the way. However they mean to handle the logistics, some men want their women to come to bed with their shoes on.

Garter belts and stockings are, however, more popular. Lingerie is the number-one turn-on for men, and black the preferred color, followed closely by red. They like women to come to bed wearing silken pieces so they have the privilege of removing or working around them.

"My wife has some silk G-strings," a man in his late twenties writes. "I love to eat her out while she's wearing one. I push the silk aside with my tongue. By the time she has an orgasm, the silk is wet, and I like to rub my penis against it awhile before I pull the G-string off and fuck her."

Another man says, "I like to see a woman in something trashy now and then, like those bras from Frederick's with the nipple holes cut out. It only works if the woman is classy and you have to ask her. I get a thrill out of bringing her down to my sexual level."

Like many men, this one apparently believes we exist on a higher moral and/or sexual plane than he does. Perhaps his desire for "dirty" sex practices expresses the hidden wish to see a woman as someone other than a madonna.

Whatever the reason, some men want us to be less pristine. They ask:

Why does she shower before I eat her out?

"*I like the taste and smell of natural woman. I especially like to smell the creases of her crotch, if it's been a hot day and she's been sweating. This is an incredible turn-on to me, but she thinks it's dirty, so she bathes,*" writes a Seattle salesman.

Some men find the natural musky smell and taste of our vaginas, even armpits, arousing. They wish we were slightly less clean, but we are conditioned to find our (and his) natural body odors offensive.

Some women won't submit to cunnilingus unless they have bathed the vaginal area within the past ten minutes. This may be an expression of female self-loathing, or at least excessive cleanliness.

"I wish gals could compromise on this a little," says a pro football player. "I don't want a gal who hasn't had a bath in days, but I am turned on by the combination of her natural odor and a good perfume, used lightly. I prefer to make love to a gal hours, not minutes, after her shower. By the way, I am always clean when I have sex. Men don't naturally smell as good as you gals do."

Other men want us to flaunt ourselves in public. They ask:

Why is she such a prude about being seen?

"I like to make love in our backyard on summer nights. She worries the neighbors will be peeking out their windows. I say if that's all they've got to do, let them look. She won't even answer the door in her short shorts. I'm proud of her body and I wish she didn't treat it like it belonged to a nun. Am I crazy to want to show her off?" writes a Nevada insurance agent.

Sex in semipublic places is high on the male wish list. They want to do it on the balcony or patio, in bathrooms or closets at parties, in your childhood bed while visiting Mom and Dad. What's a close second to the fantasy of intercourse on a plane or train, a *Forum* readers' favorite? Having her perform fellatio while he's driving on an interstate highway. Partly he craves the visual thrill of watching her do something she wouldn't do without being coaxed. And partly the risk of getting caught arouses him.

"I think everyone has made love in a public place once in their lives," writes a secret service agent, formerly based in Washington, D.C. "My own experience was inspired by one of the more famous Washington sex scandals. I was desperate to make love on the steps of Congress and convinced my woman to go along. She didn't wear any underwear. I unzipped my pants, sat on the steps, and she sat on my lap. She scraped her knees a little, but it was very exciting. We got a lot of sexual mileage out of that night. It was even better when we talked about it in bed than when we did it."

The favorite feminine garb for semiexposed sex is any skirt or dress worn without panties. Some men will be satisfied if you just go out with them occasionally sans underwear and save the sex for later.

"Knowing your woman isn't wearing her panties is hot," explains a midwestern man, "because it's your secret. My wife surprises me sometimes in public by telling me she's not wearing them. We went to pick up the car at the service station last Saturday. It wasn't ready, so we had to wait. We were sitting on a cheap vinyl couch in the waiting room when she whispered in my ear, 'I hope I don't sweat and stick to this stuff. I'm not wearing panties.' I got an erection that lasted the thirty minutes while we waited for the car and the ten-minute drive home. In the car, I kept my hand in her pussy, playing with her. When we got home, we fucked like crazy."

Some men enjoy having other men admire their seductively clad wives and lovers. "When my wife wears a revealing outfit to a party, we have great sex as soon as we get home," writes a twenty-nine-year-old Southerner. "Once, we didn't make it home. We had to pull off the road and fuck in the car."

And many men ask:

Why won't she masturbate for me?

"It really gets me going to watch a woman masturbate herself. That is one of the sexiest things a woman can do for a man. Yet few of the women I've been with are willing to do it. I had a lover who would look at me the whole time she rubbed circles around her clit. When her hips started grinding and her eyes got heavy, I almost came in my pants. That woman was hot," writes a chemical engineer.

We might find this one a man's most difficult request. It hasn't been that many years since women weren't supposed to enjoy sex. Now we tell women it's okay to enjoy sex as long as they're in love. Masturbation still isn't acceptable to some women, though they practice it. He wants her to do it for his erotic benefit. She's embarrassed to admit she does it at all. Masturbating for him seems a sharing of a part of her secret self, an intimacy almost impossible for some women to extend.

"Men see female masturbation as an X-rated video made solely for one person," explains the California psychologist. "He sees it as her gift to him, not an emotional sharing like lovemaking. He's more detached from the experience. The visual element of it, combined with the knowledge she is doing something uniquely for him, arouses him. He even thinks he's doing her a favor by encouraging her to masturbate for him; he's helping her to let go, which men think women can't or don't do often enough."

You may not find all, or any, of these practices erotically palatable. Perhaps understanding the reasons behind a man's request will encourage you to be more adventurous, and perhaps not. Don't tell him he's weird, sick, disturbed, perverted, or otherwise out of his mind because he is aroused by something different than you are. Everything we've discussed in this chapter is the sexual equivalent of mocha-double-nut ice cream. It may not be vanilla, but it isn't beyond the spectrum of "normal" either.

What You Need to Consider About Arousal Variations

- .They are *not* fetishes. A fetish is usually one part of the female anatomy or one specific item of clothing upon which a man's arousal is totally and exclusively dependent.
- They can arouse you, too. Treat his request as a sex game.
- They are neither painful nor illegal. So what can it really hurt to try them once?
- If you absolutely don't want to do it, you can say no without feeling like a prude.

11 Is It Tough Enough?

....

"Nobody considers it a problem until you can't get an erection. Then it has a name: impotence. What they don't talk about is the state between not getting it and getting it right, getting it hard. I call it the bends. I am very aroused, but my erection is not hard enough. You could bend my cock in the middle. This happens to me a lot more now than it did five years ago."

—A forty-five-year-old reader

The real man is . . . *always* rock hard. Isn't he? The macho code says he is.

It's easier to accept the fact that men often require arousal aides and practices—beyond the kissing, touching, stroking of foreplay —when you understand how important the quality of their erections is to them and to us. Hardness is one of the two criteria by which men measure their sexual potency. The other is penis size. They put size first, hardness second. We can't do anything about his size, but we, or he, *should* be able to do something about the quality of his erection.

"I know women go for hardness; and they think a semisoft cock is a negative reflection on them," says David, a former Chippendales dancer. "If they weren't as hung up on hardness as men are, they wouldn't prostrate themselves over a soft one like they do. Now that I'm over thirty-five, I find my erection comes and goes during lovemaking. My partners have trouble dealing with it when it goes a little soft. Their reactions range from 'You're seeing someone else, aren't you?' to 'Maybe it's true what I've always heard about guys like you being secretly gay.'

"But it wouldn't be fair to criticize women for their attitude about cock strength without admitting I panic, too, when it gets soft. I probably transmit my concern to them. The other sex tends to believe what you believe about yourselves. We buy into a lot of women's myths about themselves and they do ours."

So many men have written asking me how women feel about the quality of their erections that I was somewhat surprised with my survey results: less than a third of the respondents said they were occasionally dissatisfied with the quality of their erections. The majority of these were over thirty. This small group, however, expressed the same fears I've heard.

They want to know:

How hard does a woman need a man's cock to be?

"My erections are never rock hard. Sometimes I can only penetrate a woman initially if she sits on me. After we fuck awhile, I can hold it inside her in any position. Before I shoot, I feel good and hard, at least to myself. Some women have commented on this problem, though they were quick to reassure me it didn't bother them. If they didn't care, why mention it? Is there a standard for hardness? How do you tell if you're off?" writes J. G. in Maine.

The degree of firmness he describes should satisfy his partner's desire for penetration. Though he can help her achieve orgasm without an erection, they both would obviously prefer that he have one, at least most of the time. I try to allay men's fears about size and hardness, but I don't believe they always accept the words of solace. Fifty women can tell a man the size of his penis or the quality of his erection doesn't really matter, and he will still have doubts.

Alan, a sex therapist, agrees: "Women's assurances don't do much to ease men's fears and frustrations about size and erectile hardness. She can swear he's virile; and he won't believe her. He'll think she's being kind. His thinking is, if she loves him, what else would she say?"

Men have been given few examples of a satisfying sexual encounter with a limp penis. (Other than *Coming Home*, in which Jon Voight played a wounded Vietnam vet, I can't think of one.) Their erotic literature and ours features the stone penis. The erotic hero's organ is rarely shown on video in less than a solid state. How could anyone miss the connection between hardness and male sexuality?

"You only read about the softer penis in the Your Problems and How to Solve Them sections of the sex books," says a twenty-nine-year-old manager. "My erection already isn't as tough as it was when I was nineteen. Some days it's weaker than others. On those days I feel old."

Realistically one could expect a man's erection to vary in quality depending on many factors, including illness, stress, fatigue, medication, drugs or alcohol—the same factors determining whether he will have an erection or not. His rapport with his partner also plays a role.

"The quality of my erection varies proportionately to the person I'm with," writes a thirty-nine-year-old from the northeast. "If that person really excites me, it is solid and doesn't go down until orgasm. If she doesn't, I won't get as hard. My penis usually falls out and goes flaccid and we have to resuscitate it, which is annoying. You can't have good sex when you're annoyed. Maybe you shouldn't have sex with a woman unless she really excites you, no matter how attractive or available she is."

Maybe he shouldn't. Certainly we shouldn't assume we aren't attractive because he doesn't want to have sex with us, or because he doesn't achieve erection.

Men also ask:

Why don't I stay hard throughout intercourse?

"I try to hide it from my partner when my erection begins to decline, but it's hard to hide something like that. I pull out of her and go down on her. Or I fuck her from behind so I can hold the base firmly and thrust with my hand. I'd rather be able to fuck hard and steady as long as we both want me to. What can I do to get it back?" writes a thirty-five-year-old Philadelphian.

Men fear losing the solid erections of their youth as much, or more than, we fear the physical signs of aging on our bodies. This man's partner might consider him the greatest lover she's ever had. She would probably be surprised to know how much he worries about the changes in his erectile hardness during lovemaking. Oblivious to his fear, she may be effusive in her praise of him. He's still grieving over the loss, barely hearing, or ignoring her praising words. Or worse, she may worry about the "problem" as much as he does.

In *Sexual Solutions: A Guide for Men and the Women Who Love Them*, Michael Castleman says, "Some women get upset if their lovers' erections subside during lovemaking. Many men—and women—blame themselves if their lover seems less than passionately aroused. If a man's erection subsides, the woman may fear she no longer excites him or that she did something to turn him off. This may be the case. . . . Frequently, though, erections subside on their own for a while."

Some men blame themselves; others blame their partners.

"I haven't got it anymore," laments a forty-three-year-old from Atlanta. "I used to wake up with an erection so hard it felt like I could hammer nails with it. No more, babe, no more. Now I'm like a pro athlete the first year off the team, going a little soft. It lets me down sometimes right in the middle of fucking. I guess you could say I let myself down."

A Connecticut man takes the opposite viewpoint: "I've been cheating on my wife for the past year. I started seeing other women when I had trouble staying hard while we made love. It made me nervous. Was it me or was it her? I guess it was her. The other women make me hard."

Perhaps the male midlife crisis is triggered in part by erection changes. I hadn't considered that before one man pointed out the connection to me: "Nobody, male or female, would have a midlife crisis at all if we didn't see physical changes in our bodies we don't want to see. Sure, there's the existential 'Is that all there is?' question playing in the back of every intelligent brain. Don't tell me the question couldn't be ignored until we were on our deathbeds if our bodies didn't let us down, forcing us to think about aging and dying.

"For women, the turning point comes when looking in the mirror.

It's the face that gives her away to herself. For men, it's the mighty penis, which isn't so mighty anymore."

Most of us, male and female, work through the crisis and, we hope, come out on the other side as more fully realized adults. But don't expect him to have an easy time handling a difference in his erections that may even seen negligible to you. His fear of going soft—of losing his manhood and disappointing you—is at the bottom of his requests for the arousal practices that may seem upsetting or offensive.

How Not to Handle the Situation

- Don't tell him he's hard if he isn't.
- Don't tell him it doesn't matter to you that he doesn't get as hard as he once did—unless he asks.
- Don't expect reassurances will make him feel better. Good sex will, over the long haul, take the edge off his discontent. Don't be afraid of inventive sex that may increase his arousal, but don't make his arousal an obsessive goal. Take your own pleasure. Nothing excites a man more than pleasing his partner.

Part Four

PERFORMANCE

The Quickie: The Ultimate Male Experience?

....

"Not only are we expected to be sexually knowledgeable without having received adequate instruction, but we are expected to perform flawlessly at every sexual opportunity . . . never default, never fail to perform."

—Barry McCarthy in *Male Sexual Awareness*

The quickie no longer constitutes an acceptable male sexual performance.

Pre–Masters and Johnson and the squeeze technique, men presumably cared only how many times they had "it," not how long "it" lasted—and "it" was intercourse. Not that they didn't want to please a woman, but scoring was the game. They thought either she didn't need or want sexual pleasure, or she had all the satisfaction she could handle in the often brief encounter with him.

"Come to think of it," my sixty-year-old friend Gil says, "there wasn't as much pleasure in sex for men either. It was over too soon for anybody to have a good time. 'Wham, bam, thank you, ma'am' was how people fucked when they were too embarrassed about sex to make love."

He may be in his "declining years," Gil says, but he has experienced more sexual pleasure after the age of forty than he did before. Like the men who have written to my columns and those who responded to my survey, Gil wants more from sex than a quickie. In fact, many men want lovemaking, including intercourse, to last much longer than it does. Sometimes they kid themselves about how long it actually does last. And sometimes they berate themselves for not achieving a sexual Olympian time goal.

The men I surveyed said intercourse should last anywhere from ten minutes to several hours, with the majority (51 percent) preferring twenty to thirty minutes. But they said in their experience it rarely did last so long, which isn't surprising considering the average length of intercourse is five to ten minutes. Several wrote to tell me they "blamed" only themselves for not lasting long enough. ("It's a man's job to last. A woman can keep going for hours. He lets her down if he doesn't hold up a good while.")

They have internalized the post—sexual revolutionary myths: A real man *always* has unending staying power, and all women are capable of multiple orgasms achieved during sustained sexual marathons.

These sexual myths are no more realistically achievable than the others. A real man *always* is ready to have sex and he *always* has solid erections. While increased sexual knowledge should have made sex better for everyone (as it did for Gil) by showing us the possibilities in lovemaking beyond the quickie, the information explosion has unfortunately also increased the pressure on most men. Performance is now a double-edged equation: his erections and her orgasms. He relentlessly measures and counts the pieces of his manhood on both sides.

In *Male Sexual Awareness*, McCarthy says, "For many men, sex is a bluff, a desperate struggle to maintain the image of the infallible 'male performance machine.' When sex becomes so competitive, so performance oriented, there is little room for pleasure. . . . A good lover is not a technician; he is someone who can enjoy and be involved in the feelings of tenderness, intimacy, and emotional expression that occur during sexual interaction."

Intellectually, men know this. Emotionally, they have trouble accepting it. When sex isn't good, they are more likely to blame themselves than us. They remember the negative comments a woman makes about their lovemaking as if the words had been branded into their flesh.

"I know sex isn't supposed to be a performance," one man wrote, "but I can't help acting as if it were. When a woman wants to talk about sex, I cringe inside. She probably wants to tell me what she needs sexually, and I'm supposed to be enlightened about that. But I'm embarrassed I didn't know it already. I did something wrong. My performance was off. I'm afraid she's going to give me failing grades. I will be humiliated. Once a woman told me I lasted too long and asked me, 'What are you waiting for, a train?' "

According to McCarthy, "The worst fear I've seen in men has been the fear of humiliation by the woman. This fear of being humiliated is more prevalent than the fear of a non-functioning penis. . . . Though I don't think it happens much in reality, it's a real fear."

That fear is the basis of his performance anxiety. If all he wanted were a quickie, he would never feel anxious. He would care about only one set of statistics: his. But he wants a lot more, for both of us.

12 Foreplay, Not for Women Only

•••

"I would love a woman occasionally to make love to me. Take me into her arms, kiss me passionately, and lead me into the bedroom. From there, slowly remove my clothes, kissing and caressing each part of my body as the clothes come off. One time a woman did something like that to me. She started at my feet, kissing and sucking my skin. Up she went, past my calves and knees and in between my thighs. I had an incredible erection. She went past my genital area and started at my navel and worked her way down. I was going crazy. Finally, after a good while, she grasped my penis in her hand and started kissing and sucking. It was all I could do to keep from coming. Now that is foreplay!"

—A thirty-nine-year-old Philadelphian

Foreplay is a negative word.

As Shere Hite said in *The Hite Report*, "It brings to mind the sex-manual blueprint for sex . . . as if making love were a game in which the major objective is to move on to 'the main event,' intercourse and penetration."

Foreplay has come to mean the sexual work men do for women to prepare us for intercourse. The assumption is that he doesn't need any preparation. One man described foreplay as "the period in which she holds him off while he revs her up." Is something missing here?

Men certainly think so. I've received more letters from men who want more touching, stroking, kissing, sucking, and loving than from those who want more of the exotic sex practices. About half the men in my survey said they did not get as much reciprocal foreplay from their partners as they would like. Another 35 percent said they were pleased with the attention they were getting.

Only 15 percent gave what we assume is the standard male response: He doesn't need it, thank you; intercourse is enough for him.

"Sometimes she reciprocates," a forty-two-year-old New Yorker writes wistfully, "but I wish she did more often."

The idea that foreplay isn't "necessary" for him is a natural outgrowth of our belief that he is *always* ready for sex. We often treat him like an overheated motor on the verge of sexual explosion. If we fondle him too freely, he might reach orgasm "too soon" or outside the vagina, which he "shouldn't" do. Many women believe his need for more touching before sex indicates their lack of sex appeal. ("My wife's idea of foreplay for me is taking off her clothes.") Maybe if we tossed out the word "foreplay," we would be less rigid about lovemaking.

In *Sexual Solutions*, Michael Castleman says, "A widely held notion about lovemaking is that it is divided into three distinct stages: foreplay, intercourse, and afterglow. The very word 'foreplay' suggests that it happens before the 'real thing.' However, the idea that foreplay precedes actually 'doing it' is an indirect cause of many men's sexual difficulties. There are no such things as foreplay and afterglow. There is only *loveplay*."

Men *do* want more from sex than intercourse and orgasm. The question they've most often asked me is:

Why doesn't she touch me more often?

"Contrary to sexual stereotypes, I seem to enjoy more foreplay than some of the women I've known. I wish women understood men also need tenderness and affection in bed, plus leisurely, extended forms of foreplay. I want her to run her hands all over my body, especially my back. I want her to lick my ear, kiss my hair, play with the hair on my chest. I want to be stroked," writes a forty-year-old college professor from the northeast.

Men ask for the same kinds of physical affection we enjoy. Many report their nipples are sensitive, particularly to licking, kissing, and sucking. They like to be rubbed all over their bodies with long, slow strokes. Yes, they even like to be hugged.

"Women hug back, but they don't hug," complains a twenty-six-year-old. "They hug other women, children, old people, and dogs. But they seem to think real men don't want hugs or quiche. I guess men are part of the problem, and that includes me. I want to be hugged and held and stroked. Yet I don't ask for it. I'm afraid of sounding like a woosie. Women can say, 'I need a hug.' We should be able to say it, too."

They also would like more genital play.

"I've been with women who grasp my penis as a signal they're ready," writes a forty-five-year-old chiropractor from Memphis. "Except for the one good tug or two, they don't touch it unless it falls out during intercourse and has to be reinserted. I've also been with women who lavish attention on the penis and balls, but somehow make you feel they're doing it to prove their expertise. The women I love best play in bed.

"They touch me all over my groin area, penis, balls, anus, and the sensitive place between the anus and balls. Often they lick and kiss, too, but not always. Sometimes they just play with their hands, and it's nirvana. I love it."

When they don't get the kind of touching they want, men often blame themselves for not communicating their needs, as the man quoted above did. While they admit it's "silly," "a mistake of pride," or even "dumb" to suppress their requests for touching, they do remain silent. A Chicago attorney sees it as "the reverse of what women do. They are embarrassed to ask for what they need in terms of genital contact leading to orgasm. We are shy about asking for simple physical affection. It doesn't take a rocket scientist to figure out why. We're stuck with our own myths and stereotypes, aren't we? Each sex gets half a loaf and covets the other half, when we could be sharing the whole thing."

Or men blame themselves in another way. They believe women really cannot touch them without fear of orgasmic explosion.

"In the past I have come too soon when a woman devoted a lot of erotic attention to me," says a thirty-five-year-old. "I can see where they hold back from touching because they want to save the man's orgasm for later. It shouldn't make any difference who comes first, because a man should continue pleasuring a woman after his own. But it does make a difference. Women are disappointed if you come too soon. A lot of them are embarrassed about being the sole focus of attention. They feel like you're watching them come, and they don't like it."

Another man said: "Women feel like exhibitionists if they're out there on the passion limb alone. You come too soon, you let them down. You become a voyeur. So they're afraid to touch you too much, afraid of setting you off."

Many men, however, say their orgasms haven't been *that* easily triggered since they were in their early twenties.

"I can handle a lot of touching, genital and nongenital, without exploding into orgasm," writes a thirty-two-year-old Philadelphian. "I am sure most men can. If genital play gets me dangerously excited, I can move her hand. Ask her to stroke my body for a while instead. Going back and forth from genital play to overall body stroking prolongs lovemaking for me."

And Gil, my sixty-year-old friend, says, "One of the joys of aging is discovering you can hug and kiss, full naked body to full naked body, without worrying if you'll come on her thighs."

The other question men often ask is:

How can I get her to touch me the way I want to be touched?

"*I particularly enjoy having my balls played with. Few women do this. Probably they think the balls are too sensitive. They must be handled gently, but they can be handled. I've asked women to do this, and they roll them back and forth in their hands a few times or maybe plant a kiss on them and quit. I also like it when a woman inserts a finger in my anus. I'm afraid to ask for that because they might think I'm queer,*" writes a Southern business executive.

The obvious, easy answer to any "How can I get her to . . ." question is: Try asking. Men don't, however, ask easily. Just as we believe men can be manipulated into behaving the way we want if we learn the right tricks, they believe women can be encouraged to give them what they want sexually if they learn the tricks. You would think people living in a society that accepts "communication" as the answer to every problem would have learned to talk in simple sentences by now, but we haven't. Asking for something makes one vulnerable.

Though they rarely ask, many men enjoy having a woman play with their testes. Sensitivity varies with each man, and so does his concept of "play." One man writes, "Having my balls sucked for several minutes while she works her finger in and out of my asshole is tremendously exciting." While another says, "I like to have my balls gently massaged; it's not an easy technique to learn."

Women often do avoid this part of the man's anatomy for those very reasons. It's sensitive. Each man wants something different. And none of the techniques for handling them seems to come naturally.

"What every man is secretly hoping, of course, is that she'll ask him exactly what he wants to hear," says Alan, a men's group leader. "In the five years I've been working with men's groups, I've heard men say the same thing over and over again about the kinds of sex they want or want more of. The sentence begins, 'I wish she would . . .' But does he share his wishes with her? No. He acts like the wishes will be magically fulfilled as long as he doesn't articulate them.

"If she asks, he's eager to show and tell her how to please him. I would advise a woman to lick his balls, lightly, experimentally, then cup them gently in her hand and ask him what he'd like her to do with them next."

You might wonder why the same man who asks you to masturbate for him has so much trouble requesting simple affection or telling you how to fondle his testes. Men have difficulty asking for anything that could be considered a "foreplay" need. It may appear to you that either sucking his genitals or masturbating yourself achieves the same end: his arousal. He sees it differently.

"Men are supposed to ask for sex, not affection," Alan says. "They are expected to request exotic sex practices, not simple hugging and fondling."

Men are reluctant to make specific genital requests for other reasons, too. ("I don't want to call attention to my small cock by asking her to touch it.") And many men do enjoy having a woman finger their anus, but they think she'll associate the practice with "something dirty" or "homosexual love." The area is sensitive, psychologically as well as physically.

"I love having my ass touched, the cheeks caressed and nibbled, my anus tongued and finger-fucked," one man writes. "I love it, but I don't ask for it because women are so sensitive to the fact that you might be a bisexual these days. A sensitive male ass is associated with homosexuality."

Not surprisingly, men want extended loveplay as much as we do. They frequently ask:

How do I prolong foreplay?

"Contrary to the stereotype, I find some women are more interested in cutting to the chase than I am. They want enough foreplay to get hot. Then they want me to suck or masturbate them to orgasm, then fuck them. I would like to extend the foreplay, maybe suck a little, then go back to slowly exploring each other's bodies. When a woman holds your head vigorously between her legs, it's hard to change the subject," writes a northeastern professional man in his thirties.

Men do not hold exclusive franchise rights on goal-oriented sex. Many of us believe sex has a point—and the point is to have at least one orgasm and preferably more. A surprising number of men have told me their partners now expect a first orgasm, achieved through oral sex, mere minutes into the love play.

"Women are better sexually educated than they were twenty years ago," writes a forty-two-year-old ad agency owner. "I was out of circulation for fifteen years, and that's the biggest difference I see on reentering the dating scene. They know what they're entitled to and how to tell you to give it to them."

Another "reentry male" has also noticed the difference in his partners now and those of a dozen years ago, but he attributes the change to another factor: "I am sleeping with women who are over thirty now and more sexually self-assured. They don't take as long to get aroused as younger women. That's good and bad. The bad part is they tend to rush you through the amenities sometimes. If you'd told me twenty years ago I'd be moaning over the shortening of foreplay now, I wouldn't have believed it."

And one more perspective: "I'm married and my extramarital fucking around is with married women. We don't always have time for foreplay. And often we don't need it because we've been fantasizing the encounter for hours, even days in advance. We start on sizzling. It's different from married sex."

These men all have valid observations about the changing sexual scene. Women are more sexually goal-oriented than we once were. We also know how to get our goals met. As we age, we do respond more quickly to erotic stimuli than we did in our twenties. However, most of us, male and female, would like lovemaking to last longer than it does, at least part of the time. And sometimes men are counting on us to slow it down.

What to Remember About Foreplay

- As a word, it's not accurate. As a concept, it's counterproductive. Consider the whole experience loveplay. (We keep forgetting sex is supposed to be fun.)
- Don't be afraid to touch him. It is highly unlikely that he will explode on contact; and if he does, it is likelier he will want, and be able, to do it again.
- Ask him how he likes to be touched.
- If he insists "foreplay" is for women only, relax and enjoy.

13 Clitoral Stimulation Anxiety

●●●

"Yes, of course I can locate her clitoris. What man would admit he couldn't find one? If he really can't, he must be pretty inexperienced. Yes, of course, I know how she likes me to touch it, hard and fast until I bring her off."
—A thirty-seven-year-old executive

If she really enjoys having her clitoris pummeled, she is the rare woman. More likely, he has targeted the general area of the clitoris, where he applies his stimulation efforts. (Also possible: She fakes orgasms.) The vast majority of women prefer indirect clitoral stimulation in the form of relatively gentle circular motions with hand or tongue. Imagine the clitoris as the point in the center, the movements rhythmically surrounding it. This is what women like and usually need to achieve orgasm. Many men are still confused both about the location of the clitoris and how to touch it.

"Heavy hangs the clitoris over the penis head," writes an illustrator from the southeast. "The clit has had more publicity than Princess Diana. It is also more revered. We worship it, even if we aren't quite sure where it's hiding, slippery little love button."

This bemused approach to the subject doesn't quite hide the writer's sincere confusion. Like half of the respondents in my survey, he reported his partner was capable of achieving orgasm through intercourse alone. ("Hand or mouth stimulation of the clit area isn't always necessary," one man writes. "If she's hot, when I pick up the pace and ram it to her, I can bring her home.") In her classic study of women and sex, *The Hite Report*, Shere Hite found only 30 percent of women capable of achieving orgasm during intercourse without direct clitoral stimulation. A definite disparity exists between the reports of men and women.

The letters I've received as a columnist indicate that the clitoris continues to be somewhat of a mystery, in spite of the multitude of articles and books explaining its location, significance, and touch requirements. Men are understandably unsure of how to proceed because:

- Women have faked orgasms with them, leading them to believe those who can't achieve orgasm without clitoral stimulation really can.
- The hidden location of the clitoris lends significantly to its aura of mystery.
- Men fear being too rough or not firm enough in their approach.
- And, perhaps most significantly, they fear a woman's need for clitoral stimulation indicates they are not manly enough to satisfy her with the penis.

This last is their version of our myth: A real woman should reach orgasm via intercourse alone. As long as we deny our needs to ourselves and our lovers, the myths continue to flourish. And deny (or suppress) we do. Over half the men in my survey reported their lovers did not tell them how to stimulate her clitoris. My mail has consistently shown the same results.

Not surprisingly, men still ask:

Is there a foolproof method for locating the clitoris?

"Every woman I've been with has responded differently to my touching her in pretty much the same place. I'm beginning to think I don't get it right on every one of them. Some women have a noticeably hard little knob; others don't. Am I not sufficiently exciting the ones who don't? Or does the location vary somewhat on different women?" writes a twenty-eight-year-old from Atlanta.

Shere Hite also found that men have problems locating the clitoris. Admitting they do is, however, equivalent to a woman publicly confessing she has never had an orgasm. Few are so honest. Over 90 percent of the men I surveyed said they knew exactly where it was. ("I know where her clitoris is; she likes me to fuck it easy, then hard.") In some cases, their replies to the follow-up question on how she likes him to stimulate it persuaded me he wasn't precisely on target. ("She likes a good pinch, then a massage.") Others seem to have a clearer understanding. ("She does not desire direct contact with her clitoris—prefers in the area, i.e., clitoral hood, etc.")

"It's usually at the top of the vagina, just below the pubic mound," writes a business consultant. "But it is small. I have trouble finding it in my current partner, though no trouble with other women in my past."

The "foolproof method" for locating it is simple: Ask. Or, take her hand and say, "Show me." Yet many men feel uncomfortable asking a woman for specific directions to any part of her anatomy, or for suggestions on what to do when they find it.

"I wish women would show you what they want," a chemical engineer from Los Angeles writes. "I have a basic approach, which is pulling away the fleshy part of the labia with one hand and wetting my index finger and alternating between a circular motion and a back-and-forth motion. I figure that way, I won't miss anything. But I would as soon a woman guided me by taking my finger and showing me just how and where she likes it and what kind of pressure she prefers. When women do that, I feel more sure I'm getting it the way they want. Everyone's different."

Yes, everyone's different, but men do look for that "basic approach," which will work, more or less, for all women.

They ask:

What kind of clitoral stimulation do women want?

"Some will guide you, but many act like you are supposed to know. I use my tongue a lot in long slow strokes running horizontally along the sides of the clit, and that seems to work for most women. Is there a particular tongue or finger technique they prefer?" writes a Texas reader.

The majority of my readers and survey respondents believe women prefer oral stimulation to manipulation by hand. Or perhaps they were more confident of their oral abilities.

"Lubrication is very important in this delicate procedure," writes a divorced northeasterner. "Even if you lubricate your hand, it may not be enough, especially if she doesn't get wet right away. That's why the mouth works better. Women love to have their clits licked and sucked. I love doing it, too."

And a southwestern editor says: "I can definitely turn her on with my tongue. I'm not so sure about my hand. She says she likes the pressure different than I usually do it. I have trouble finding the right degree of pressure. Sometimes she says I am too gentle. Hands are rougher than tongues, so it's hard to know."

But some men do report manual stimulation is as effective as oral. ("She likes me to kiss her on the mouth while I play with her clit. You can't have your mouth in two places at once.") Others consider a combination of the two methods most effective.

"This works on nearly every woman," writes a divorced corporate president in his forties. "I make soft circular motions with my middle finger very wet as I kiss my way down to her stomach. Often I roll her over on her stomach as I kiss her back while still making the motions with my finger.

"What excites my latest lover particularly is playing with her clitoris while having two fingers pumping her vagina while biting her ass. Last night as I bit, sharply sometimes, she squirmed and moaned a lot, and my thumb found itself resting against her anus. I pushed my thumb as I bit and she pushed hard down onto my thumb. I then slipped her leg over my head, keeping two fingers and the thumb working, and licked and flicked her clit with my tongue, finally sucking it into my mouth, with pressure, sending her into multiple orgasms."

In their quest for the "right" clitoral techniques, some men, like the one above, are bold and inventive. Others fear causing pain or discomfort and move in exaggeratedly slow and gentle fashion.

"I touch her clitoris very, very gently," says a junior-college teacher. "In fact, she likes me to caress her around it since just barely moving the surrounding area makes her feel very good. She is so sensitive, she does not need direct clitoral contact. Merely brushing lightly against it with tongue or wet finger is enough to cause orgasm."

Some of these men appear to be quite confident of their mastery of clitoral skills. Their lovers, they say, seldom if ever guide them, but they don't seem bothered by that. ("I get my directions from her body's responses. When I'm in the right spot and moving it the right way, she's wigging out.") Many other men would appreciate a little direction.

"This is probably the most important part of pleasing a woman; and it's shrouded in mystery," writes a Connecticut man on his third marriage. "I've never been with a woman who reached orgasm without direct clitoral stimulation—though my first wife didn't tell me the truth about this until years later. Obviously it's key. Why don't women let us know exactly how they want this done? In the past I have sometimes felt like I might have given a woman more pleasure than I did if she'd guided me a little."

Given the confusion surrounding the clitoris, men not surprisingly want to know:

Why does she need clitoral stimulation in addition to intercourse?

"Don't think I am one of those black men who doesn't like to eat a woman out. I love the taste and smell of pussy. No inhibitions here. I like to bring my woman to orgasm first with my tongue or hand, then fuck her. But I don't know why she needs continued hand stimulation to come again during fucking. Is this the way all, or most, women are made?" writes an artists' representative from Los Angeles.

Hite discovered that the "overwhelming majority" of men she polled would rather their partners reached orgasm through intercourse, without additional manual stimulation. Though they do understand the sexual biology behind their partner's needs, most men would probably rather she didn't require the extra touch during intercourse. They want penile thrusting to be "enough" for her, as it is for them. That does not make them selfish. Woman's clitoral-stimulation need is a relatively new development in the history of sex, and too many women have expected men to get the information from any source but them. And even if you are clear about your needs with a man, the women in his past might not have been.

"I can bring any woman to orgasm with forceful thrusts of my cock," writes a thirty-four-year-old attorney. "Of course I know women need direct clitoral stimulation, but I give it to them by the way I fuck. Hard genital contact is all it takes."

Early in my sex-advice-writing career, I was tempted to respond to such remarks with indignant and scathing comments. Then I realized the man was only partially responsible for his attitude. Blame his partners for their share in creating that oversized penile ego. Apparently none of them has told him that hard genital contact is not "all it takes."

"I was married for ten years to a woman who wouldn't talk about sex," says a forty-year-old from the South. "My first lover following the divorce educated me on the clit. I noticed that when we made love, she put her hand between our bodies and rubbed herself. It bothered me that she did this. I asked her about it, and she explained she needed this to reach orgasm. I was thirty years old and I felt like a kid in school. No wonder my wife had never wanted sex."

The myth of the penis as ultimate satisfier dies hard. In mainstream erotica and hardcore porn alike, the hero always carries the heroine to a higher level of ecstasy than she's ever known on the strength of his penis. He may have brought her to orgasm via cunnilingus or another method before intercourse, but the main event is strictly no hands, and earth-moving.

Over half the men in my survey reported that neither they nor their partners manually stimulated her clitoris during intercourse.

"I do it sometimes, but it doesn't turn her on," writes a twenty-nine-year-old. "Sometimes she takes my hand away. Once she said she wanted to feel me as close to her as I could be while we made love, and the hand kept our bodies apart." And later: "I am not sure if she comes during intercourse or not."

A thirty-six-year-old manufacturers' rep says: "I've had over twenty partners since I became sexually active. I can remember two, maybe three, who used their hands to stimulate their clits while fucking. Most women in my experience don't. Nor do they ask for it. I would be happy to do it if they wanted it."

Some men believe their partners neither want nor expect to reach orgasm during intercourse—lending reinforcement to the theory that erotic pleasure in post–sex therapy America has become a your turn–my turn proposition.

"My wife wants hers before we fuck," says a Philadelphian. "The question of stimulating her during fucking doesn't come up, unless we are doing it doggie style, which I like but she doesn't. Then I play with her clit from behind so she's getting something out of it."

And a New York restaurateur says: "I've given up on the idea of giving my wife an orgasm during fucking. She doesn't get off this way. She gets off other ways. It bothered me for a long time, but I've adjusted. I'm forty-eight. I came of age on the concept of the simultaneous orgasm. This woman is half my age, but I guess she knows what she wants and how she wants it."

Others say manual or oral stimulation before intercourse arouses their partners sufficiently so they can reach orgasm during the act.

"The trick is to bring her to the edge of climax, then stop stimulating her with my hand or mouth and start fucking her," explains a Midwesterner. "She's so hot, the pressure of our bodies grinding against each other brings her off. It's a matter of timing. I prefer doing it this way at least part of the time rather than bringing her off through cunnilingus or a hand job—though she doesn't care how she comes as long as she comes."

However he handles the issue in bed, a man probably does feel somewhat uncomfortable with the fact that she doesn't reach orgasm through intercourse. Often he blames himself for not being able to "give" her orgasms this way.

"In the beginning my lover had orgasms during intercourse," writes a twenty-eight-year-old southeastern executive. "Now she doesn't. I come. Then she masturbates herself while I kiss and caress her until she comes. I blame myself for this. Maybe I don't last as long as I did. I should be able to give her at least one orgasm during intercourse. She doesn't have trouble having orgasms. The trouble must be me. I'm coming too fast."

Or more likely, she didn't tell him what she needed until they were established as a couple. Many women fake orgasms in the beginning of a relationship because they're too embarrassed to admit they require direct stimulation. Later, it's even harder to admit they lied. If a man told her what he was thinking now, she probably would tell him the truth.

But the truth doesn't always protect a man's feelings either.

"I hate to admit this, but I don't like it when my partner stimulates herself during intercourse," writes a Chicago businessman. "I feel like I am not necessary to her pleasure if she can give it to herself. She has explained to me why she does things this way. Of course I understand the mechanics behind it. I know about the clitoris. I consider myself an informed man. I still have trouble with it. I'm glad, however, that she was doing this from the first time we made love and assured me she's always done it with every partner. It didn't just come out of nowhere."

Perhaps he would feel better about her lovemaking requirements if his were the hand doing the stimulating.

"I want to make contact with her clit while we're fucking," writes a northeastern executive. "It makes me feel closer to her. If we're doing missionary position, it's absolutely necessary that I masturbate her at the same time. In female superior, she and I both sometimes play with her clit. She puts her hand over mine or vice versa, which I find very sexy."

A man's attitude, positive or negative, toward manual stimulation during intercourse is based on two factors: His belief that he *should* be able to satisfy her with his penis and that there is something unnatural about her release if it's obtained otherwise; and his past experience with women and specifically whether they were honest with him or not.

You Can Make Him Feel More Comfortable About Clitoral-Stimulation Needs By

- Asserting it from the beginning.
- Or, confessing your earlier clitoral "lies" by assuming responsibility for lying, not casting blame on him for not satisfying you.
- Sharing the statistics with him so he won't believe you and he are not normal.

14 His Sexual Style

••

"You could call me a cocksman and proud of it! Women say they don't care about size. They claim they want sensitive men. They swear they don't care about orgasms, it's the 'closeness' they want. Balls! Women want cock. They want it big, thick, hard, and long lasting and handled by a real man. They're just too nice to say so."

—A Texan

Not every man is so besotted with his penis as this Texan. He is the personification of the macho code. Apparently he's found enough machisma sweethearts to make his philosophy work—or at least prevent him from having to question it seriously. While all men are affected by the code, few live it to this extreme.

But every man has a sexual style, a way of making love that is influenced by whether he believes he can satisfy his partner largely via his penis, his technique, or his attention to romantic details. His style is really the embodiment of his sexual attitudes. It will or will not be changed depending on his experiences.

All men are capable of being good lovers—or not so good ones —regardless of their style. Even men with serious sex problems can make wonderful lovers. You will find men who can satisfy you in every category. But if you are like most women, you consistently choose your lovers from among one general type. There's nothing wrong with that—unless you're repeatedly disappointed or hurt by your experiences. The answer does not lie in "changing" him. Only he can change himself, and he may not do so at your request.

The penis-centered man puts all his faith in his penis. He asks:

Why doesn't my wife have an orgasm while performing fellatio?

"Other women I've been with have gotten as much from sucking my cock as I have from being sucked. I am unusually large, which women find very pleasing. Does her failure to respond sexually to cocksucking indicate a problem between us? I think this might be her way of expressing unhappiness with me in other areas of our life together, but she says no. She just doesn't get off on sucking cock," writes a twenty-seven-year-old Midwestern husband who refers to himself as "Hung Dog."

While many women enjoy performing fellatio, and for a variety of reasons, a rare few reach orgasm via this route alone. Yet some men think they should. Like the writer above, they fear her failure to do so is an indictment of them as lovers and husbands, or worse, as "cocksmen." It's a "love me, love my penis" philosophy that is not nearly as arrogant and selfish as it sounds. His ego is heavily invested in his male appendage. He walks as if an invisible weighted line connected to his penis were pulling him forward. His identity as a sexual being rests largely in his penis. Think of him as a gambling man who bets the farm every time he makes love, and you will have a good insight into how your responses to his penis affect him.

In fact, there's a little bit of the penis-centered man, the personification of the macho code, in every man. You aren't going to get along with him if you don't love his penis, too. On the other hand, you shouldn't ever conceal your needs from any man, or play up to his ego, whether it's located largely in his penis or elsewhere. What women sometimes don't understand is the difference between trying to change a man to suit them and telling him what their needs are so that he can accommodate them.

"I thought my cock was enough to satisfy any woman until I met Angela last year," says a thirty-five-year-old. "Why wouldn't I think that? No woman before Angela said otherwise. I had trained myself to last a long time during fucking. What more could a woman want? When she told me she couldn't come unless I ate her out or played with her clit while we fucked, I was insulted. I thought she was a man-hating bitch. She said my idea of foreplay was unzipping my pants and pulling out my cock and letting her admire it.

"I'm not sure how or why we decided this relationship was worth pursuing, but we did. I learned how to give her what she wants, and she turned out to be the most wildly exciting and responsive lover I've ever had. She makes me feel like she loves my penis after all. Now I wonder what was really going on with the other women."

It is difficult for a man who believes he should be able to satisfy any woman with his penis to admit otherwise. A woman like Angela is certainly the best incentive. Some men haven't been lucky enough to be challenged by such a woman.

"I was married for five years when I discovered that my wife masturbated herself to orgasm after I fell asleep," writes a Colorado developer. "She went into the bathroom, locked the door, and put a towel against the bottom of the door so I wouldn't hear her. Usually I am a sound sleeper. On this particular night, the phone rang, wrong number, waking me up. I didn't know where she was, went looking for her, found the door locked. When she finally opened it, she was crying and she told me what she'd been doing. I felt like someone had kicked me in the balls. It couldn't have been worse if she'd been fucking some guy in there.

"It all spilled out then. She said she almost never had an orgasm during lovemaking. She said it was my fault because I didn't touch her the way she needed to be touched. You know what bothered me most, aside from the fact that our whole sex life had been a lie? She had a pet name for my penis. She called it 'The Satisfier.' Maybe it was her private joke."

Other men believe technical proficiency is the criterion for being a good lover. They frequently ask:

Is there a technique for bringing a woman to the edge of orgasm and keeping her there for a while?

"I have a small cock, so I rely on superior technique to please my partner. I want to give her the best experience of her life, a long slow buildup with the resulting orgasm harder and longer than anything she's ever felt. I have noticed it is possible to vary the length and quality of my partner's orgasms depending on the position and hand or mouth stimulation accompanying it. But what will keep her from going over the edge until I want her to do so?" writes a newspaper reporter.

Many of the questions I've received have been technical in nature. The overwhelming majority of men are concerned about giving their partners pleasure. Some believe a combination of superior technique and self-control will put any woman in erotic heaven. Ironically, the most extreme examples of the type are the men we often consider too coolly controlled to be great lovers. They are erotic performers, not full participants in lovemaking.

Maybe you will have more sympathy for him if you understand that his technically proficient, yet detached lovemaking style is engendered by his need to please—and his belief that only an exceptional performance will do that. He may also be compensating for a small penis, which he has, or thinks he has. By holding back his orgasm for as long as possible, he thinks he is giving you more than other men do.

"I think every time should be great sex," says a thirty-nine-year-old management consultant from the northeast. "At least you should be striving for this each time you have sex. Foreplay must include touching, licking, kissing of her entire body, with special attention paid to licking of the labia folds prior to cunnilingus, followed by a '69' with me performing oral sex on her until she reaches orgasm. Lovemaking must include several positions, preferably ending with the doggie style if she is not receptive to anal sex. She must climax at least once or the sex will not matter. I will not be satisfied."

This man is more goal-oriented than other men. He believes every woman can have multiple orgasms if he pushes the right buttons for her. Approaching sex like a work project, he has a plan for how the encounter will be played out. He assumes full responsibility for the sex, whether good or bad.

"I think performance is the most important part of sex," writes a forty-four-year-old banker. "And that is the man's job. In my experience, women care more about performance than penis size. And women now are more knowledgeable about sex than they were when I was first dating. They have plenty of basis for comparison. If you don't tongue them the way they know they can be tongued, they won't respond for you. I am not blaming them or saying this is bad. It is the natural result of a freer society. It places more burden on the man, who must always be conscious of his technique."

Some men believe a repertoire of positions qualifies them as expert lovers. As if they had cut their teeth on the *Kama Sutra*, they make love all over the bed, floor, sofa, kitchen counter.

"I amazed a partner recently by bringing her to orgasm while fucking her with one foot on the floor," confides a northeastern sexual gymnast. "I began from a kneeling position on the bed, then without removing my cock from her or losing the fucking rhythm, I moved her to the side of the bed so that I could keep one foot on the floor while I pounded away at her. Women like variety and the sense of being pulled bodily from one position to another as they're being fucked.

"Because I am tall, I can also sit her bare-assed on the kitchen counters and fuck her standing up."

In truth, most women would find this man's gymnastic abilities exhausting as a regular routine.

"I prided myself on fucking in several different positions each session," writes a Midwesterner, "until I met a woman who told me it would be nice to leave the gymnastics to Ringling Brothers once in a while. I got the hint. I was doing it because changing positions helped me control myself better. When I got close to coming, I switched positions. The break did it for me without her knowing I needed it to maintain control.

"But maybe women don't care if I pause. At least that's the impression I'm getting from women now."

A man who believes technique and control are the criteria by which he is measured isn't likely to confide his reasons for frenetically shifting positions or relentlessly insisting she have an orgasm before he does. Even the man above, who was affected enough by this woman's comment to modify his lovemaking style, probably didn't tell her his original motive for developing that style. Sharing such information would be admitting his "performance" is a carefully staged and delicately balanced operation. It would make him vulnerable.

The best way to handle him is to tell him what you need, without attacking or questioning his style.

Perhaps the most difficult lover is the "romantic," who believes passion, not clitoral stimulation, causes orgasms. He often asks:

Why is it so difficult to romance the modern woman?

"I am thirty-eight years old, lost my virginity at twenty-seven, have had only one partner in my life, not counting prostitutes, whom I use now. Some months ago we broke up. I have as strong a sex drive as any man, but I don't want to get into a relationship with a woman based on sex alone. Women act like something is wrong with you if you haven't made a solid pass at them after several dates. How do you woo a woman today?" writes a northeastern computer softwear engineer and consultant.

Nearly 20 percent—a surprising number—of the men I surveyed did not lose their virginity until they were at least twenty. Not all this group struck me as romantics, but many did. A late first experience isn't the only indicator of the romantic. Some men who lost their virginity in their teens have the same "romantic" attitude about women and sex. They are the pedestal builders, the men most prone to divide the female sex into madonnas and whores.

There is a touch of romance in every soul, but these men take it to the extreme.

"My wife was rummaging through my desk and found my American Express receipts from business trips. She was shocked to discover I use an escort service, which she knew was a euphemism for call girls. She says she will do anything for me that those girls do. All I have to do is ask. But I can't ask her to let me fuck her ass or come in her mouth. How do I make her understand I want some things she shouldn't have to do?" asks a Midwestern executive.

Yes, some men still think like this, and they aren't all over fifty. They are tormented by a narrow vision of humanity in which all men are too bad for good women. The prostitute is as much his punishment as his release. You might be able to enjoy sex with him as the wicked other woman in his life, but as his wife, you will find erotic adventures limited.

But you don't have to marry him to know it will be this way.

His sexual style is evidenced by his courtship behavior. He is the attractive, "incurably romantic" man whose quest for the right woman has led him through many dates that didn't end in relationships. His misty-eyed "I think I finally found her" phase disintegrates quickly into mistier-eyed sadness. He praises lavishly, touches sparingly, and makes frequent deep eye contact.

The secret to having good sex with him is being someone else.

"My wife occasionally dresses in sleazy lingerie, the kind you buy at Frederick's of Hollywood," writes a Southerner. "With it she wears a feathered mask that we bought at Mardi Gras on our honeymoon. I can do things to her when she's dressed like that that I can't do otherwise. Is this normal?"

"Normal" is, of course, what we say it is. Most men want to be both normal *and* the best lover you ever had. No matter what his lovemaking style, he wants to know:

What makes a man the best lover a woman ever had?

"I want to know what to do and how to be so I can give the woman I love the best sex of her life. She is a warm and responsive woman and relatively easy to please sexually. I give her orgasms, but I would like to give her more. She is open to trying new things. In your experience, are there some ways of making love and certain male sexual habits that women associate with the best?" writes a Michigan systems design engineer.

Any woman with a reasonable amount of sexual experience has a favorite lover or two. She probably considers (or remembers) him as "the best" she's ever had. Men both fear they're the man who came after the phantom "best" and desperately want to become the "best" lover in her life. They don't understand that for the most part, we reserve the designation for men who have moved us emotionally as well as physically. Penis size and technique, erotic or romantic, take second place to the indefinable X factor—which is part "chemistry," the mix of extreme desire and strong attraction, and part "intimate knowledge," the result of two bodies who are attuned coming together.

You can't plan on having that kind of sex, but men try. They give a lot of thought to what constitutes such an experience and how they can bring it to the women they love. Without doubt, they believe the larger responsibility is theirs. (Great sex is more what they do to and for us than have us do to them or with them.) They rarely believe they are "the best," but they're always striving to be.

"Personally, I enjoy extended lovemaking, up to three hours if I can do it," writes a twenty-six-year-old northeasterner. "The best experiences include getting in the shower together. I love fucking under running water. But only if I know she is enjoying it and is fully satisfied, do I think it's great sex."

And from a midwesterner, age thirty-nine: "Intensity makes sex better than good. Pleasing my partner makes it great. I enjoy driving a woman over the edge. I literally want her to ask me to stop."

A forty-seven-year-old middle manager: "Great sex is a complex combination of caring feelings, 'hot' kissing, certain perfume and bodily smells, sexy clothes to see, touch, and remove, extensive buildup of tension, and real concern for each other's feelings. And most of all, she enjoys it more than she ever has with any other man."

Others defined great sex as:

"A warm, tender moment of sexual love climaxing superb sexual technique on my part."

"A feeling of closeness, then making her go crazy during sex."

"Her being wildly ecstatic, me being able to keep myself on the edge of an orgasm for a long time."

"Twenty-four hours alone with someone I really care for—not all that time spent fucking, of course."

"Total sexual connection. When we're both in a groove, when our bodies lead and our minds follow."

"Knowing I have fully satisfied her, body and soul."

Very few men in my survey defined great sex in terms of their own pleasure. Only one man, who claims to have had over five thousand partners, gave the kind of answer you might expect: "Nonstop, all night, with lots of ladies, until we faint or fall asleep."

No matter what their sexual style, most men want their particular way of making love to move you as no man has. Knowing this should make it easier for you to tell him what you want.

What You Should Notice About His Lovemaking Style

- How it correlates to his life-style. For example, the overly fastidious man who won't sip from your glass of wine probably won't perform cunnilingus with joyous abandon either.
- How it reflects his attitudes about women in general.
- How amenable he is to building some adaptations into his style. (If he never can allow you to assume the lead, he isn't.)

15 Faking, Nice or Nasty?

•••

"While I was filling out your questionnaire, I casually asked my wife of two years if she'd ever faked an orgasm with me. She calmly said, 'Sure.' I said, 'How many?' She said, 'I don't know. Several.' I said, 'Anytime recently?' She said, 'Last night.' I felt like she kicked me in the balls. I'm supposed to trust this woman more than anyone else in the world?"
— A northeastern corporate attorney

I doubt if there exists a literate man who does not know that women can and do fake orgasms. Some of those men will swear no woman has faked with them, and more will be equally sure *this* particular woman hasn't faked with them. The facts don't support their convictions. Less than a third of women reach orgasm via intercourse alone. Far more than a third of men believe they have brought their partners to orgasm via intercourse alone. Apparently a lot of women still do fake.

Like my column readers, the men in my survey are cognizant of the reality that is often at odds with female sexual performance. Approximately 40 percent said women had faked orgasms with them. Another 40 percent were not sure. Only 20 percent swore none of their partners had ever faked. On the whole, the majority 90 percent were at least somewhat bothered by a parter who had, or maybe had, faked an orgasm.

A Midwestern salesman writes, "I don't honestly know if any have faked or not. If you can believe them, they've all said they came. There is no way a man can tell for sure unless he's performing cunnilingus. You can feel the quivering with your tongue. Otherwise, you have to take what they say on faith."

And a high-school football coach from the South says: "I was easily fooled with a lot of twisting and hollering when I was young.

Now I'm not that easily fooled, but I still wouldn't bet a woman couldn't fake me if she wanted to. If I found out she was doing it, I'd break up with her."

Nothing hurts a man as much as having his partner tell him she has consistently faked. Often, he considers himself a sexual failure. Faking is such a hurtful issue, most men avoid it by not asking, while others almost demand repeated reassurances.

Perhaps that is why men have so often queried:

Is it better to ask "Did you come?" or not ask?

"When I was married, I thought I knew if my wife came or not. I didn't ask. When we were getting divorced, she told me she often faked in order to stop fucking because it wasn't going to get her anywhere. Now I want to be sure my partners are satisfied, but 'Was it good for you?' sounds so corny. Also, I feel like I should know without asking. Do women think you're insensitive if you have to ask?" writes a forty-year-old from Washington, D.C.

Other reasons are cited by the experts for the increase in cunnilingus, but in my opinion, the main motivating factor is: He can be sure her orgasm isn't faked if he "gives" it to her orally. Many men dodge the question "Did she or didn't she have an orgasm during intercourse?" by satisfying her orally first.

"I figure if she fakes the second one, it's not so bad," says a twenty-four-year-old. "At least I'm sure she got something. And I hate asking. You feel like such a jerk asking."

Whether they articulate the philosophy or not, men believe a real man should know how to satisfy his woman, and by extension, he should know if he's done it or not. He shouldn't have to ask.

"If you ask her later, that implies you didn't know what to do for her to give her an orgasm," says a thirty-nine-year-old. "You blame yourself for not knowing. So even if you think she's faking, you go along. You don't ask. If you ask, you have to deal with the fact you didn't know how to do it for her."

Some men ask, but doubt the answers.

"When I've asked, no woman has said no," writes an Atlanta businessman. "I had my doubts in some cases as to whether they were telling me the truth. Two women told me, 'I think I came.' Now I'm sure they couldn't have come. If a woman doesn't know if she's come, she couldn't have, could she? I mean, she should know. It's not a great feeling for a man to hear that from a woman. It's sort of like having her say, 'I think I felt your penis in me, but I'm not sure.' "

And a local television-news anchor observes: "Twenty years ago when I was starting out in the world as a lover, you would never ask her how it was for her. You just assumed—hoped and prayed, really—it was good. Then we all got smarter. You learned it probably wasn't good for her, just as you'd suspected it wasn't. Now you ask. You hope and pray it's as good as she says it is, even as you're suspecting it isn't. We've come a long way, babies."

Some men do understand the woman's position: she knows how disappointed he will be if she tells him she didn't have an orgasm. Maybe she didn't even fake one, but let him assume she'd had one, too. In that case some men think asking her forces her to lie. He asks.

"It's putting her on the spot to ask," says a telephone lineman from the South. "No man really wants to hear she didn't. Sure, you want her to be honest, but do you want her to be that honest while your cock is still slick with her juices? No, you don't; and she knows it. I don't ask. If it's an ongoing relationship, I try to talk about it when we're not in bed. It's easier on both of us."

The majority of men are looking for foolproof ways of gauging whether she did, or did not, reach orgasm so they won't have to play inquisitioner.

Their question is:

How can I be absolutely sure she came?

"When my tongue is on her clit, I'm sure. Otherwise, I'm guessing. Aren't there definite physical signs of orgasm that all women exhibit? Or can a woman have the indications without the release? I admit I'm confused. I tried to get through Masters and Johnson, but I couldn't," writes a southeastern marketing director.

Many men consider the signs of female arousal—erect nipples, shortened or heavy breathing, elevated heart rate, increased vaginal secretions—proof of orgasm. Conversely, they say they knew she was faking when:

"Her nipples were soft. All other partners had hard ones."

"She was too dry inside."

"All noise, but her breathing and heartbeat weren't elevated."

Some men expect to feel the contractions of her vaginal muscles when she reaches orgasm, and assume she didn't if:

"No internal twitching. All the writhing was external."

"Felt no internal convulsions, nor the muscular tightening and release that comes with orgasm. Besides, she was a lousy actress."

No man in my survey mentioned the "sex flush," the red rash covering the breasts and shoulders of women in the postorgasmic phase. Many of my column readers, however, have written to say they consider this rash the definitive proof of orgasm. (Some say this is why they prefer the light on.) Others concede that all the physical indicators, even the flush, could appear on a woman who had *almost* reached orgasm as well as one who had.

"A man in tune with his woman should know," writes a twenty-eight-year-old husband. But other husbands have been surprised to learn they'd been fooled. Married or not, a man who discovers a regular partner has been faking is usually distraught. He asks:

Why would a woman fake an orgasm with her man?

"It's like lying to him. I can see faking with a guy you don't know well, if the sex wasn't that great and you didn't want to be with him again. Then, faking could be considered a polite way of getting out of something you wish you hadn't gotten into. But why lie to someone you love? What's the point?" writes a self-employed southwesterner.

Women fake on an occasional basis as a means of ending sex we weren't that excited about having—or to "reward" him for his efforts, even though they didn't result in orgasm. Almost every woman has faked an orgasm once in her life because she didn't, or couldn't, say no, to sex. Another group of women fake regularly because they don't know how to tell him they were faking in the beginning. This is the self-perpetuating fake: she never tells him what she does need to reach orgasm. Therefore he can't give it to her, and she continues faking. According to my mail, it still goes on.

Unfortunately, the woman in this situation grows increasingly angry at the disparity in sexual pleasure. Eventually her repressed rage erupts, and she tells the man she's been faking all along. He is understandably crushed. His reactions include:

"I felt angry and impotent."

"She told me during an argument. I felt like punching her lights out, but I'm not that kind of guy."

"Depressed and unloved."

"I felt lousy. What had she been doing, 'pity fucking' me for the duration of our four-year relationship?"

"I couldn't get it up with her anymore. I believe a man's performance is directly related to the attitude of his woman and the degree of intimidation he feels with her. There's nothing more intimidating than hearing you can't please her and you were too dumb to know it."

"I felt stupid. She must have been laughing at me inside."

"Insulted. It's a very demeaning way to treat a man."

He's too hurt to analyze her motives in a rational way. When he asks himself the question, "Why did she lie?" the answer often puts her in the worst perspective. Men say:

"She obviously wanted me for something other than sex. Money. I'm sure it was money."

"She was using sex to get me to marry her, and she didn't even enjoy the sex. Why would you want to marry someone who couldn't bring you off in bed? This is why men don't trust women."

"I think women who fake don't like sex very much, or they don't like men, or both."

Few men understand as well as this New York computer analyst: "If a woman fakes, then there is a strong reason for her to do so. I don't feel I'm necessarily the cause of it. Even if she did say I was the cause, how can she be so sure? I doubt one man can be totally to blame if she doesn't have an orgasm. It's usually a combination of many reasons."

Or this railroad employee from Texas: "I would bet all women have faked at least one orgasm in their life. Most women shelter a man's ego—in the sense that they portray their lover as sexually fulfilling for them. And are we glad they do! If women didn't protect men in this way, a large percentage of the male population would be a little more humble about their abilities as studs and lovers."

Most men say they prefer the truth to a good fake. Yet some now admit to faking orgasms, too. This surprised me when men first wrote to me to share their own faking experiences. I'd always assumed it was something they couldn't pull off. They can.

Occasionally they ask:

Do women have any idea that men can fake orgasms, too?

"*I have done this on a few occasions. Each time I was with a woman I didn't enjoy that much. She wanted sex, and I obliged her. Getting it up is one thing; getting it down another. When I could see I wasn't going to be able to ejaculate, I pumped in and out fast and hard, then gasped and moaned and jerked around as if I'd come. If a woman is plenty juicy, from eating her out and her own arousal, she won't notice your missing ejaculate. Or will she? Were these ladies merely too polite to say?*" writes a northwestern gentleman.

Other men who have written to explain how they faked an orgasm cited a similar scenario. She had initiated sex, and he, rather than admitting he was too tired or not particularly interested, had allowed himself to be seduced. While he was able to achieve and maintain an erection, he wasn't able to ejaculate. Because he had assiduously applied himself to performing cunnilingus, he assumed she wouldn't notice he hadn't ejaculated during his performance.

In other words, men just can't say no, either.

According to Levine and Barbach in *The Intimate Male*, "The major reason most men faked orgasm was to conceal their macho vulnerabilities. With sex roles continuing to shift and more women initiating sex, men are finding themselves in uncharted waters. No longer are they the sole sexual initiators who determine when and where sex will take place. Since a macho man is still expected to be ever ready for sex, men are beginning to find themselves in the uncomfortable position of being pursued by women when sex is not foremost on their minds. Consequently, men who don't find their partners sexually attractive or who are not particularly aroused at the moment are put in the age-old woman's role of faking or having to learn to say no."

The overwhelming majority of men who admit they have faked an orgasm did not do so with a regular partner. ("You can satisfy your regular partner, then quit without explaining it, or just by saying 'I'm too tired to come tonight.' ") But ending the encounter this way left them feeling vaguely uneasy. They hope she's fooled, but they haven't fooled themselves. Their lack of desire might even embarrass them.

One man writes, "I faked an orgasm once, and I felt like I was less than a man with that woman. We'd had sex once, and it was great. I was looking forward to seeing her again. She called me at the office before I had a chance to get back to her, and asked me to come over after work. When I got there, it was clear she wanted a repeat performance. I wasn't quite psyched up for it because my mind was on a problem at work. Her menstrual period was trickling to a close, and she, of course, had to be honest and tell me that in advance. Everything worked together to turn me off, but she wanted sex.

"I don't know if she knew I faked it or not, but I never called her again. I still feel a little embarrassed when I think about that night."

While they ascribe less altruistic motives to the female faker, they say they are sometimes too gentlemanly to let the woman know they didn't have an orgasm.

"Men are supposed to have one every single time or something's really wrong," writes a Midwestern guidance counselor. "Naturally a woman assumes she's the problem. She thinks she didn't turn you on enough. Faking gets you out gracefully—or so the theory goes. I've only done it three times. The third woman called me on it. She put her finger in her vaginal juices, tasted and smelled it, and said, 'No way, José.' I felt like a jerk."

And another man caught in his lie by a similarly suspicious woman says, "There's a lesson in this for everyone: Don't fake. You do the thing you think is least offensive and it turns out being the most offensive, hurtful thing when you get caught."

I agree with him. Enough distrust between men and women exists already. Why build more?

The Bottom Line on Faking

- Don't.
- And if it's done to you, don't take it any more personally than you would want him to take it if you were the performer, not the audience.

16 Limited Performances

....

"I would like more anal sex. That feeling of tightness gripping your penis is like no other. It's great. The thrill with anal sex is the same every time, like penetrating a virgin."

—A thirty-eight-year-old newsletter editor

Anal sex and fellatio top the male sexual wish list. Many of the letters I've received at *Penthouse Forum* and *Penthouse Letters* have been from readers eager for advice on how they can get their partners to accede to their desire for these and other beyond-basic sex practices. My survey respondents also said they didn't get enough: anal sex (50 percent), fellatio (75 percent), cunnilingus (55 percent), variety in positions, practices, etc. (40 percent), multiple orgasms (25 percent).

Women complain in our magazine surveys that we don't get enough variety or oral sex. Rarely, however, do we protest we aren't getting as much anal sex as we would like. That and the desire for fellatio culminating in ejaculation are primarily male wants. Some women are openly hostile to both practices.

Men know we are hostile, and sometimes they think they know why. "Women hate mess," one man explains. Others cite our fear of doing anything we consider "dirty," "unnatural," "immoral," or "potentially painful." They are sure they can overcome our objections if we'll let them try. ("I know she'll love being fucked up the ass, if she'll only give me the opportunity to prove it to her," insists a twenty-seven-year-old newlywed.) No wonder they so often ask:

How can I get her to try anal sex?

"In other areas, she is adventurous and uninhibited, but she guards her asshole like it's been blessed by the pope. I have promised to use plenty of lubrication and move very gently, taking it at her pace. I want her ass so

bad now I have trouble thinking of anything else when we fuck. When I see her ass, the cheeks round and muscular and high, I want to part those cheeks with my cock. What can I do to get her to open her magic hole to me?"

I advise men who want anal sex (or any other sexual practice) badly to let their women know *how* intensely they desire it—and back the request with reading material, a book or article that might help allay her fears as to the cleanness or morality of the act. As this man has, a man should promise to take it at her pace, and arrange a signal word that, when spoken by her, means unequivocally, *go no further.* ("No" doesn't always work, because some people in the heat of passion cry out no or oh no, when they mean yes.) Then he must also offer her something in return: the fulfillment of her number-one sexual wish.

I do think a woman should try to accommodate her beloved's desire—and he, hers—unless circumstances make it difficult for one to do so. (Men who have large penises, for example, realize that anal sex isn't something they will practice often in life.) Trying it once or even occasionally may not meet his frequency desires, but an ongoing sexual relationship involves some compromises on both parts. Besides, part of the appeal of anal sex is the infrequency with which one is likely to have it.

"If we had anal sex regularly, it probably wouldn't seem as exotic to me as it does now," admits a forty-seven-year-old Philadelphian. "I want more of it, but if I had more, wouldn't I want something else?"

Another man says, "I had to overcome her objections to anal sex on the grounds of dirty and painful practices. When I convinced her it wasn't dirty as long as you didn't take your cock out of her asshole and put it into her cunt, she agreed to try. To her surprise, it wasn't that painful. To my surprise, it wasn't as big a deal as I thought it would be. Maybe I needed her to do it to prove she loved me."

Men may no longer use "proof of love" as a reason for requesting women to go to bed with them, but perhaps they reserve the label in their minds for certain practices. ("I wanted her to do anal sex with me, because she'd never done it with anyone else. I wanted to be that special to her.") And most do associate anal sex with a close and intimate relationship. A few men said they "think less" of a woman who submits to the practice too soon in a relationship. ("If she'll let me plumb her asshole before I know her, I think she has no self-respect.") Others say anal sex requires a greater-than-average degree of trust and mutual knowledge, and the woman who submits too soon probably trusts too easily.

"My wife and I don't do it very often," writes a Connecticut man. "When we do, I feel particularly close to her. It's a weird kind of intimacy, partly based on her assuming a very female, very submissive role in the lovemaking. But it gets us both hotter than normal fucking does. She has intense orgasms anally, though she won't want it at all unless she's in the right mood for it. Like I said, it's weird, but it's great, and not something you do every day."

Some men also enjoy anal stimulation. They like having their partner insert her finger into their anus while she performs fellatio, or during intercourse. More men would ask for this if they weren't afraid of being considered homosexual.

"I love to have my asshole licked and fingered," writes a northeasterner, "but I rarely ask for that. Because of AIDS, women are sensitive to anything they might interpret as a clue to bisexuality. I have to know a woman well and trust her before I confide my desire for this."

Another man adds: "Being anally stimulated has connotations of passivity. Everyone, male and female, has a passive side. But today men are afraid to show ours because the women who said they wanted it have changed their minds. Now they assume you're gay if you express passivity."

The other avidly desired form of loveplay is fellatio. Though homosexuals do it, too, fellatio is not as strongly identified with them as anal sex is. Some men think there is nothing more manly than ejaculating into a woman's mouth. And they ask:

Why does she get angry if I come in her mouth?

"It can't be the taste. She sometimes jerks me off because she likes watching

me shoot—and licks the remaining come off the tip of my cock. So what is the problem? I love the feeling of power you get shooting down a woman's throat. It's like nothing else."

This man sums up the basic male argument for oral ejaculation: It gives him a sense of power. Often he believes the act of swallowing symbolizes the strength of her love for him and/or his power over her. A few men even consider "swallowing" degrading to women and won't ask their wives to do it.

One man wrote: "I have a performance problem with being fellated to orgasm. I can't come in a woman's mouth. It doesn't seem right."

The pleasure in fellatio is more in the experience itself than the ejaculation. ("Ejaculation feels the same in a mouth as in a pussy; what feels different is sucking and fucking.") And the majority of men would be happy with more fellatio, whether or not it ends in oral ejaculation. In fact, many prefer not to reach orgasm this way. They understand a woman's objections, which include:

"If I thrust inside her mouth hard enough to ejaculate, I would choke her."

"Having a man come in her mouth must make a woman feel powerless. I think the thrill of fellatio for them has to be the sense of erotic power over a man. If she knows he will shoot anytime, perhaps gagging her, she loses control of the situation. It isn't as much fun then, is it?"

They would like to make it as much fun for us as possible, for obvious reasons. Men have asked me if there is an oral technique a woman can use that will prevent her from gagging. (Sometimes women write asking the same question.) I advise them to have her place the penis to one side of her mouth rather than the center, or hold the shaft in her fingers as she takes it into her mouth. Either approach prevents the penis from going deep enough to trigger the gag mechanism. These techniques also allow the woman to maintain control. As the man above noted, we enjoy performing fellatio more if we do have a greater sense of control.

What men seldom understand is that some women refrain from fellatio because of performance anxiety, not distaste. While men say they would like to get some direction from their partners on performing cunnilingus, they seldom tell women how to do what they want sexually. And contrary to the myth that says "You can't do it wrong," every man has his own preference regarding oral stimulation. Some like having the head sucked, for example, while others find the sucking action almost painful. Rather than telling her what's wrong, a few men will pull away, leading her to believe she can't please him orally.

"It's difficult to tell a woman how to go down on you," says a twenty-four-year-old salesman. "You're glad she's got your cock in your mouth. You don't want to make her mad or scare her off by saying, 'Now here is how I'd like her to suck me.' "

More often, the complaint is time, or the lack of it, rather than technique. "She doesn't do it long enough," men say. Because women do fear their partners will ejaculate too quickly, we stop fellating them sooner than they would like.

"Men are to blame for this," says a forty-year-old from Georgia. "We need to communicate where we're at to our partners. If you tell a woman, 'Yes, more, please, I want more,' she will oblige you, as long as you have proven she can trust you not to turn the encounter into a blow job. When I think I'm getting too close to ejaculating, I take my woman's head in my hands and tell her I need a little break. We will do something else for a while, then she will go back to fellating me if I ask her to. Also, I love eating her out and never stint on giving her a fair share of oral pleasure. Maybe men who don't get enough don't give enough either."

While some men define oral sex as fellatio only, most men also practice cunnilingus because they like pleasing their partners. Some even prefer cunnilingus to fellatio. I've received many letters asking:

Why won't she let me eat her out?

"I love eating pussy. It really turns me on. I love the sight, taste, and smell of female genitals. To me, they are beautiful, and each one is different. I have ejaculated while performing cunnilingus—that's how much I get into pussy. So what's wrong with my new woman? She should be enjoying the hell out of me. But every time I put my head between her legs, she pushes me away after a few good licks."

Contrary to what women believe, the mail from men who passionately love female genitalia greatly outnumbers that from men who find them aesthetically unappealing. Shere Hite found over half the men she studied rated cunnilingus their second favorite sexual activity, after intercourse. My survey results also showed men are eager participants in this form of loveplay. None of the men who filled out the questionnaire mentioned a distaste for cunnilingus. While that is probably an unusual response for a group of a thousand, I do believe men love the vagina more than women do.

"I love giving a woman oral sex, and I do not get enough opportunities to enjoy it," writes a northwesterner in his late twenties. "I love the taste and texture of a woman's pussy . . . all those secret folds and lovely passages. I also love the way women respond. My current partner sometimes reaches orgasm when I manipulate her clit with my nose while licking her inner lips."

And from a man in his forties: "As a woman responds to cunnilingus, her lips swell. She opens up like a flower. And she begins to exude a heady perfume that drives me wild."

And some men value cunnilingus as a means of strengthening the intimate tie, like this thirty-five-year-old, who says: "Couples usually don't get oral until they know each other sexually. Then I feel cunnilingus deepens a woman's trust in a man. It brings them together in a special way no other kind of sex does."

Some men perform cunnilingus the way most women do fellatio: to please their partners only.

"My tongue is not an erogenous zone," writes a thirty-seven-year-old actuary. "I don't get excited from touching my tongue to her clit. But I do get turned on by her excitement. She loves it. I can make her come over and over again this way, and that makes me feel great, like a powerful lover. Besides, I love pleasing her."

A few men have said they don't like the taste or smell of women's genitals. But more say it's their partners who aren't comfortable with their own natural odors during sexual arousal.

"I love to eat a woman out," says a twenty-nine-year-old. "I had one lover who wouldn't let me. She insisted on performing fellatio, but she wouldn't let me eat her. She said she couldn't believe anyone would want to 'stick his nose down there.' We didn't last long."

Next on the male sexual wish list is more variety. They often ask:

How can I get her out of this sexual rut?

"I love my wife. She will not do anal sex. Rarely will she give me head. We have straight sex. It's good, but it's like having apple pie and vanilla ice cream every night of your life. I've had affairs with other women, and twice she's caught me at it. She thinks I'm seeking the excitement of a new woman. It's only partly that. When I cheat on her, it's with a woman who will do the things she won't."

"Why doesn't he tell her that?" was my first response to the many letters I received from men citing their frustrated need for sexual variety as a reason for having affairs. I thought the wife, or partner, should know how much he wanted the kind of sex she refused to have. But here's what some men said in response:

"I'd been married for six years when I had my first affair. During that time I'd asked her for anal sex, more oral sex, more of any kind of sex!—more times than I can remember. I can't believe she didn't know I wanted it."

"Shouldn't she be able to figure it out?"

"I didn't tell her I was seeing another woman strictly for the kind of sex I got there because I didn't want to make her competitive. Do you think I'd feel good about her finally sucking my cock because she found out another woman had?"

"I didn't want to turn it into a threat situation: give me what I want or I'll get it somewhere else."

Perhaps such men are afraid to touch the real issue: how much their sexual performance may depend on variety. Machismo prevents a man from confessing he needs anything more than the opportunity to perform. How can he tell her he needs more?

I'm still not sure the average woman really understands her husband is more likely to stray to find sexual variety than for any other reason. Our affairs are motivated by different reasons. We roam because we're dissatisfied with the man. Or we're looking for romance in our lives. He's probably looking for a woman who will perform fellatio for a long time.

In the beginning phase of a typical relationship, both partners will be satisfied with each other. As the relationship ages, both need some degree of variety to stimulate them, he more than she. Taken in context, it's both easy to see why he needs change and also why he might feel vulnerable in admitting he does.

Not all men connect their desire for a more varied sex life to the question of fidelity. Many try to find what they need with their partners or through fantasy. And a large segment of men say they are capable of having more than one orgasm in some of their encounters if they get different kinds of stimulation from their partners. Their question is:

Why won't she occasionally accommodate my desire for a second orgasm?

"I can come more than once if the sex includes either fellatio and anal sex in addition to intercourse. All it takes on her part is a little effort to get me hard again the second time. She can do this by fellating me and at the same time massaging the area between my balls and anus or inserting a finger into my anus, pumping it as she sucks. When I ask for this, she says she's tired or it takes too long, or the worst, that I've had one orgasm—as if men aren't supposed to get more than one!"

Many men share the belief they are being deprived of the opportunity to have second orgasms by partners who don't want to prolong lovemaking in order for them to do so. Obviously long encounters aren't feasible for every night of the week. But these men want the occasional marathon session, and now feel as entitled to it as women are to multiple orgasms.

"I know women's multiple orgasms, when they happen, tend to come closer together than a man's possibly could," a thirty-two-year-old lawyer from Colorado says. "I'm not saying orgasms should be handled on a quid pro quo basis. But if men are expected to be sensitive to a woman's desire for continued stimulation after his climax, shouldn't she be sensitive to his occasional need for a long, down-and-dirty fuck session?"

Another man says, "I think women hesitate before going on to stimulate a man again after he comes because they're afraid he'll feel pressured to perform again or won't be able to ejaculate a second time, but will drive them both nuts trying. Also a lot of us grew up with the idea a man was left hurting by an erection if he didn't ejaculate."

Some men have discovered they can entice their partners into a longer lovemaking session by giving them more attention.

"You can get almost anything you want from a woman in bed," confides a forty-two-year-old entrepreneur, "if you give her anything she wants sexually. In sex, as in life, the wrong attitude is telling your partner what she can do for you. Ask what you can do for her. She will reciprocate—unless she's a very inhibited woman."

Yet the question men still repeatedly ask is:

How can I get more sex?

"I never get enough sex in any form, fucking, anal, oral—I can't get enough. Why aren't women as horny as men? And if some women are, how do I identify them from the others?"

My readers and survey respondents are not a group of oversexed men. In 1989, *USA Today* ran a phone hotline on sex and marriage. Most of the callers were men, and their number-one gripe was: not enough sex. The same year, *The New York Times* ran an article in the science section about a University of Michigan study of men and women by psychologist David M. Buss, who found what bothers a man most about a woman is:

● *Sexual rejection:* Refusing to have sex; being unresponsive to sexual advances; being a sexual tease.

And what bothers a woman most about a man is:

● *Sexual demands:* Making her feel sexually used; trying to force sex or demanding it.

It would seem the sexes are definitely at odds on sexual frequency. Yet in 1988, the female readers of *Glamour* and *Redbook* said they weren't getting enough sex either. Obviously something is wrong here. I'm not sure I know what, but one man thinks he does:

"When women say they want more sex, they mean they want more cuddling and affection from their guy. When men say they want more sex, they mean they want to get fucked more often in more different ways—and probably by more different women. Even if they didn't want that, men would say they did."

How You and He Can Get More from Limited Performances

- Negotiate a minimum numerical requirement—for example, anal sex twice a month or a long fellatio session once a week in exchange for whatever you want sexually.
- Trade sex practice for sex practice. Leave the household chores out of it.
- No nagging or whining for more, as long as the minimum requirements are met. (Asking nicely is sometimes possible.)

17 The Number-One Performance Indicator: Her Orgasm

•••

"No man is a good lover if his partner doesn't come all or nearly all the time. Otherwise he's masturbating in her vagina."

—A reader

The baby boomers are the first generation to measure a man sexually by his partner's orgasm tally. While we have been unsuccessful in passing on many of our social and political beliefs to the next generation, we did manage to inflict this new version of the macho code upon them. Sex is no longer something a man takes from a woman, but something he gives to her. He is the provider in the sexual, as well as the economic, sense of the word.

A real man "makes her come."

Most men are keenly aware of the pressure put upon them. Even if they understand the "average" woman won't reach orgasm during intercourse, they still equate their ability to maintain a long-lasting erection with the power to please their woman. Presumably we all equate "average" with a standard we should beat. Men believe all or most of *their* partners can achieve orgasm through intercourse if they themselves "last long enough." Many regard female orgasms attained through oral or manual stimulation as either the preliminaries or additional gains, not the main event. Her orgasms and his endurance are linked in their minds.

According to Bernie Zilbergeld in *Male Sexuality*, "The real test of a good performance these days is the ability to satisfy one's partner, usually defined as giving her at least one, but preferably more, good orgasms during intercourse. With this change in definition of male sexual prowess has come first an interest, then a concern, and now almost an obsession with lasting longer."

We are still debating the old clitoral–vaginal orgasm controversy, even if we don't put it into those words. The old idea was that women should have vaginal orgasms by means of penile thrusting in their vaginas. The vaginal orgasm was, according to Freud, a "mature" response. Clitoral orgasms, by contrast, were "immature" or "infantile." In modern man's version of the story, clitoral orgasms are "average" or second best—for the most part, what other women have with other men.

That thinking puts the responsibility for good sex on the man and his penis, particularly on his ability to "last" long enough (by holding back his own orgasm) to produce the vaginal orgasm in his partner. Whether we acknowledge it or not, women understand that the pressure not only to perform but also to satisfy is on the man. If we didn't accept our sexual pleasure as largely their responsibility, would we fake orgasms rather than hurt their feelings by letting them know they didn't do well enough? If everyone truly believed women are responsible for our own orgasms, faking as a means of stroking the male ego would become an antiquated practice, like a man asking a woman's father for her hand in marriage before he proposed to her.

In the long run, assuming the responsibility for our own pleasure and accepting the power it would accord us can only make sex better for us and them. But the short-term obstacles to sexual equality loom large in many minds. If we toss out the notion that orgasms are something men "give" us, then we must "take" them for ourselves by speaking up sexually and perhaps even learning to insert our own hands between two bodies when necessary.

Some women, of course, already do that. According to my mail, the overwhelming male response to them is positive. One man writes: "When I am with a woman who is assertive about her sexuality, I relax and enjoy the sex. Women who are counting on me to make it happen for them cause me to tighten up. I don't let go until I've done right by her. It's the difference between being a

MESSAGE DE TÉLÉPHONE

À **Monique** Date **9/08** Heure **14h30** PM.

De **Louise-Anne Leblanc**

Compagnie

Téléphone **277-3154** Poste

Télécopieur

Message

		URGENT
		A TÉLÉPHONÉ ✓
		S.V.P. APPELEZ ✓
		A RETOURNÉ VOTRE APPEL
		RAPPELLERA
		EST VENU
✓		DÉSIRE VOUS VOIR

Signature

A 1630-FT

BLUELINE

solo act and being part of a duet. You don't have to carry the whole show."

Most men, however, still feel they are carrying the performance. And the majority of men do feel at least a little deflated when their partners fail to reach orgasm. A minority have convinced themselves it never happens with them. Perhaps they can't bear to face the thought of a nonorgasmic partner.

In my survey, approximately 15 percent of the men said their partners were always orgasmic. The majority, over 70 percent, said their partners were usually orgasmic, with 15 percent of those claiming they were multiply orgasmic. Again, their experiences don't quite tally with findings reported on female orgasms by Hite and others. No research studies put the number of always or usually orgasmic women as high as 85 percent. Figures vary from 33 to 75 percent.

Not surprisingly, 80 percent of the men who reported experiences with women who did not reach orgasm blamed themselves for the situation. That their partners didn't blame them seemed to make no difference.

Their comments include:

"I felt worried whenever it happened. I was annoyed with myself. Mainly I think it happened because I rushed into things."

"I had a partner who gave up after extensive efforts on my part. She said, 'You go ahead, I'm not able.' She was trying to make me feel better for my inability to bring her off."

"My current partner says she can only come through masturbation and then it takes all her powers of concentration to accomplish it. I don't know if I believe her or not. I'm willing to do anything to help a woman have an orgasm. If there is something I don't know about, I wish she'd tell me."

"She does not blame me when she doesn't have an orgasm, but I blame myself."

Is it any wonder the question men have most often asked about female orgasms is:

How can I make her come?

"I have been with women who said they had trouble coming, but I was

always able to bring them, orally, if no other way. My new woman says she rarely has an orgasm. She tells me not to worry about it, but I do. I'm sure I can make her orgasmic. The problem is she's uncomfortable with cunnilingus after a certain point. She won't let herself go enough to have an orgasm this way. Is there something else I can be doing?" writes a twenty-four-year-old.

The answer no man wants to that question is the honest one: You can't *make* any woman have an orgasm. I sometimes wonder how a woman would respond if she knew her lover had written to a sex columnist for advice on how to "make" her have an orgasm. Would she be offended by his use of the word "make" or believe, as he does, that it's the right word? Surprised or touched by his concern? Amazed he would admit not knowing anything about sex? Or shocked to discover he blames himself for what she considers "her problem"? Men rarely understand that women who seldom or never achieve orgasm do blame themselves. Such a woman secretly fears she is frigid—but he is sure he's not man enough to satisfy her.

While she seeks her own solace from various sources, including friends and magazine articles, he has few places to turn. He certainly doesn't tell his friends. When he asks me for advice, I explain the need for clitoral stimulation and suggest he get her to show him exactly what feels good for her. Some women need very specific forms of stimulation. Often I suggest he tell her what he likes sexually as a way of making it easier for her to share her desires with him. Can she masturbate to orgasm? If so, will she show or tell him how she does it?

But sometimes women either don't know, or can't or won't say.

The problem is our old nemesis, communication. Talking about sex is still extremely difficult for many lovers.

"Talking seems more intimate than fucking," writes a midwestern businessman. "You really have to let your defenses down to talk honestly about sex. It's hard to do with someone you're trying to impress. Also, both sexes believe for different reasons that you shouldn't have to talk about it. You should only do it right.

"Women keep the silence of romance. They think they should only fuck if they're in love, and if they're in love, it will happen.

Wordless rapture, like they see in the movies. Men keep the silence of the all-knowing lover. He's supposed to have the answers, not the questions."

The other side of the sexual communication problem is that we talk, and listen, too much. In lieu of personal exchanges between two lovers, we have public talk, ranging from the jock talk between men to the nongender-speak conversations Oprah and Phil have with their guests about sex. Listening to public talk has convinced us every woman can and should be multiply orgasmic, making it all the harder for one man and one woman to handle the orgasms not happening in their bed.

According to Michael Castleman in *Sexual Solutions*, "What proportion of women experience multiple orgasms? No one knows for certain, but clearly it's a minority. . . . A tragic irony of contemporary discussions of lovemaking is the amount of attention devoted to multiple orgasm, when a woman's much more typical experience is an inability to have even *one* orgasm with a man, let alone several in a row."

The second most often asked question about women and orgasms seems to follow naturally the first. It is:

Why is it so difficult for her to reach orgasm?

"I know about the clit and how to treat it. I know that women need more time to become fully aroused than men do. What I don't understand is why, after I've given her what she wants in the way she wants it, she still may not come. Why not?" writes a forty-four-year-old.

Because male orgasm is an almost certainty, men do have trouble understanding why female orgasm often remains a potentiality rather than an actual occurrence. They are particularly confused and troubled if, like this man, they believe they have mastered the requisite steps to female sexual fulfillment. It is hard for American men— and women!—to accept that not every goal can be reached by following a plan.

"I followed the directions," they say. "Now, why don't it work?"

No matter how skilled a lover he may be, there are two entities he can't control: a woman's body and a woman's mind. The female body can't be precisely navigated with a sexual road map. Some women aren't very responsive because they don't know or trust their own bodies enough to guide their man. And some women fail to respond sexually because their minds are holding them back. Women have been more sexually repressed than men in our culture, and perhaps female orgasmic difficulties are the result of that. Certainly many men have written to tell me about the problems their women have had.

"I once loved a woman who was only able to reach orgasm on rare occasions by 'riding' a towel, rolled into a thick rope, which she pulled through her legs," confides a Southerner. "She had never been able to get past her mother's admonitions against touching her genitals. (I can't begin to tell you what a wicked witch her mother was!) Her first orgasm had been accidentally reached while she was vigorously toweling herself after a bath. She was a lovely, warm, and caring woman who, sadly, could not give herself permission to be joyously sexual."

And from another man: "My wife, a former good Catholic school-girl, learned to come by lying on her tummy, squeezing her thighs together rhythmically, and rubbing against the bed. Very complicated. For a year, she couldn't have an orgasm in any position other than stretched flat out on top of me. Very uncomfortable."

When a man can see a clear connection between a woman's past history and her orgasmic difficulties, he may put less blame on himself for the situation. But he still feels sadness about what he regards as her lack of pleasure. Men want more than anything to please us sexually. And they have trouble believing women who say the orgasms aren't as important as the lovemaking. For them, this would be seldom, if ever, true. They frequently ask:

Is she lying when she says she doesn't care about orgasms?

"*Some women say it's the closeness and touching they crave, not orgasmic release, but I can't accept that. I would not want to make love without obtaining release. Lovemaking is wonderful, but orgasm is beyond wonderful. I think women just say this to spare our feelings when they don't come. It also may reflect their own ambivalence about having strong sexual urges. It sounds more womanly and loving to say it's the touching not the sexual payoff they want. Anyway, they think it does,"* writes a public relations executive from Atlanta.

She's probably not lying, but she may be denying some needs— to herself as well as him. I believe men translate some of their needs for touch into sexual ones while we do exactly the opposite. Like the Atlanta writer, I am not completely persuaded by women who claim they don't care about orgasms. How can you not care if you do or don't experience one of life's greatest pleasures? But I do understand that for some women, orgasm isn't an every-time necessity.

It is easier in our society for women to be sensual without being sexual than it is for men. We are given permission to touch, hug, and kiss our friends, male and female, and our grown children. Today, men often feel they can't touch freely. Maybe they will be considered gay. Or someone may accuse them of sexual harassment or suspect them of child sexual abuse. For us, touching is more natural than having sex, while for them, touching outside sex is neither natural nor easy.

Women do consistently tell poll takers that we can enjoy sex without orgasms and can also find sex that ends in orgasm an unsatisfying experience. (In the most recent *Redbook* survey, 60 percent of the women said they always or nearly always reached orgasm, but nearly a fourth of that group didn't rate their sex lives as good or excellent.) Many men, however, don't understand how we could rate culminating in orgasm as *not* good.

"How would you describe the worst blow job you ever had? Fabulous!" writes a New York editor. "Sex is different for men and women because we have a greater need. If we don't, they lie well. No man would ever say, 'I don't care if I come or not, honey, just making love to you makes me happy.' On a rare occasion a tired man might be content to satisfy his regular partner who happens to be ravenously horny. But, I repeat, that's got to be a rare occasion."

And a California editor says: "I've never had a bad experience in bed except with women who didn't come after I tried very hard to bring them. Even then, for me, the sex was good. I just felt bad about not being able to share it fully with them. Of course, some sex is better than others. But I think you start at good, then work up, seldom down."

Men in long-standing relationships may be more able to accept that sometimes women are content without reaching orgasm.

"My wife has finally convinced me she enjoys sex even if she doesn't come," writes a husband of twenty years. "I don't understand this, but I'm willing to accept it. Women are so much more subtle and complicated than men. Sometimes she has orgasmic experiences surpassing my own, and sometimes she doesn't come at all. If clitoral stimulation were all it takes to produce female orgasm, she would have one every time. It's more complicated."

And another husband says, "At first, I thought she was using it [her frequent inorgasmia] against me. She said she didn't need to come, which made me feel like she thought she was better than me, or her love was purer. Finally I realized she was telling me we are different both in the way we approach sex and what we need to get out of it. I know how much I need to please her. What was hard was accepting that sometimes she makes love more to please me than herself. Sometimes she has to be the one who gave."

But the men who stubbornly insist a man should be able to "make" his partner reach orgasm often ask:

How long should a man last to satisfy a woman?

"It is important to me to please my partner. I would like to go all night if I could. The spirit is willing, but etc. Some women have made me feel like I couldn't satisfy them because I didn't last all night long. I always warm up their clits first before fucking them. I have used Prolong, the cream that numbs your cock, to last longer. What I need to know is how long to last. Is there a point beyond which any red-blooded woman will have to surrender and come?" writes a twenty-seven-year-old.

This man's letter illustrates two of the most common, and damaging, misconceptions about sex:

● Clitoral stimulation is foreplay—or one uses it only for the purpose of initially exciting her.

• A woman's pleasure is dependent on a man's ability to maintain an erection for a long period of time.

A man and his partners must share the misconceptions if they believe he could satisfy them by "lasting all night." And, again, apparently none of these women have been very clear about their sexual needs—a running theme in my mail from men. This letter is typical:

"None of my partners has ever told me how to please her," writes a thirty-nine-year-old. "Do I last long enough for them? Touch them in the right places? Lord, I can only guess. My lovers aren't vocal. I wish they were. I think they must be somewhat intimidated in bed. Either that or perhaps they don't want to come off as too experienced, for fear that I might consider them 'loose.' I used to ask my (then) wife what she wanted and she would giggle nervously. She said I was doing great, don't change a thing. I hated that. It wasn't true, and I knew it. But since my wife, I have been with women who play very passive roles. It bothers me that women are so passive. That puts it all on me, to judge how much touching, how much fucking is enough."

He does not say—as most letter writers do not—how long he is able to sustain intercourse before ejaculating. Yet he is sure some magic number he hasn't yet attained will be "enough." When he reaches this point, his partner will become orgasmic or multiply orgasmic. He will have "made" her be so.

Many of the popular sex books of the past decade have promoted this idea. David Reuben in *How to Get More out of Sex* labels men who ejaculate prematurely "immature" and insists it is "the man's job" to keep the penis moving inside the vagina long enough to provide "satisfactory service to her." According to *The Sensuous Man*, premature ejaculation is "a major disaster." Even Masters and Johnson, who should have known better, battered the male in their definition of premature ejaculation, which refers to "the inability to satisfy the woman in intercourse 50 percent of the time." And we wonder why men equate sex with intercourse!

Kinsey reported that 75 percent of the men he interviewed ejaculated within two minutes. The majority of men today would consider that a premature conclusion to a pleasurable experience. (The average length of intercourse is generally considered to be five to ten minutes.) The focus of early sex therapy was on curing "premature ejaculation"—though no one ever developed a universally acceptable definition for the term. The result is both longer love-making sessions and, unfortunately, greater pressure on the man "to last."

The overwhelming majority of men are concerned about ejaculatory control and have their techniques for handling it, which include:

"I detach myself from the experience and think about other things."

"I grit my teeth, tense up, hold back. It doesn't always work. Sometimes tension has the reverse effect and makes me come."

"Early in a relationship when I'm most likely to shoot off without warning, I use the numbing creams. You don't fully enjoy the experience, but you gain control."

These popular methods of maintaining control have an obvious drawback: They force a man to suppress some of his sexual and emotional feelings for the sake of sustaining an erection. Therapists generally advise some variation of the stop-start method, which doesn't sacrifice sensation for endurance. Basically, the method involves stopping stimulation when orgasm is imminent, then resuming it as the urge subsides. (The book *Male Sexuality* has the best set of directions I've seen.)

Men who use this approach say it works well for them.

"I can control my ejaculation pretty much by alternating positions or by slowing down, then speeding up the fucking rhythm," writes a Midwesterner. "Now I can sustain intercourse for fifteen to twenty minutes, which is often more than my partner even wants."

And a man in his forties says: "Over the years I have both slowed down and developed control. I can fuck for a half an hour if I want to—and enjoy every bit of it. I like bringing myself to the edge, then pulling out of my woman and pleasuring her with my mouth or hands until I cool down, then fucking again. I've learned to enjoy the arousal almost as much as the orgasm. That's the secret."

Prolonging intercourse beyond Kinsey's two-minute mark is advantageous to both partners, but no guarantee of female orgasm.

"No matter how long I last, my partners don't have orgasms during intercourse unless one of us is playing with the clit," notes a thirty-four-year-old from Atlanta. "I like to fuck as long as possible, but I certainly don't see where it is a panacea for a woman's problems with orgasms. It isn't."

He's right. The connection between penile thrusting and orgasm is a weak one for many, many women. Extending the period of thrusting won't *by itself* bring them any closer to orgasm.

As Zilbergeld says, "It is natural to assume that a few minutes longer might do the trick (more enjoyment, orgasms, multiple orgasms) but this is often an illusion. If you can already last for ten to fifteen minutes, or even longer, the chances that your partner will become orgasmic or find more contentment if you last longer are highly improbable."

How to Lessen the Performance Pressure

- Don't equate your ability to achieve orgasm with his ability to delay orgasm.
- Take active responsibility for your own pleasure. You know what you need to reach orgasm. Give it to yourself, or show him how to give it to you.
- Create a more playful atmosphere for sex. It isn't nuclear physics.
- Praise him, but don't make the praise sound like a good grade on today's quiz.

Part Five

EMOTIONAL INVOLVEMENT

On Love and Lust

●●

"I was having lunch with a friend who was telling me he'd found a special woman. He said, 'I'm not playing around anymore.' A drop-dead gorgeous woman walked past our table. I said, 'Come on, if she told you she was ready to spread them for you, what would you say? Yes?' He responded, 'Hell, yes, in a New York minute.' That's how men are."

—Bob Berkowitz, author of *What Men Don't Tell Women—and Women Need to Know*

If the "special" woman eavesdropped on their conversation, she would be hurt. She would think he couldn't possibly love her if he talked like that. But they weren't talking about love. They were talking about sex.

Men look at sex differently than women do. We see it as an expression of love, a pathway to intimacy, a means to building a relationship and a family. They see it as . . . . sex. The old adage that men move from sex to love and women from love to sex is more true than not, at least until we reach mid-life, when women focus more on sex and men on love. Whether the critical difference between us is inherently biological or largely socially induced is, within our context of understanding male sexuality, a moot point. It doesn't matter why we're different. We are.

Men separate love and sex . . . and commitment. The joining of the three is a conscious decision, contradicting our romantic fantasy script, which says we can make him fall madly in love with and marry us if we push the right buttons. The example of thousands of "other women" who have failed to lure men away from their wives proves men can and do have affairs without falling in love.

We could learn something from the way they handle their sex lives. Women are so determined to link sex and love and commitment that we often get involved in "relationships" with men simply because we've had sex with them. (If I slept with him, I must love him.) Or we deny our sexual desires because no suitable candidate for love presents himself. (If I don't or couldn't possibly love him, I shouldn't sleep with him.) And we make ourselves crazy when a man with whom we've had sex isn't interested in having anything else with us. (Did I have sex too soon? Did I do it wrong? Why doesn't he love me after I slept with him?)

"For men, there is sex and love," Berkowitz says. "Sometimes he wants more than sex from a woman and sometimes he doesn't. He'll go after the sex as a separate issue. He might have sex with her on the first date and want to marry her six months later. Women don't get that. They obsess on controlling 'the relationship' by doling out the sex at the proper time. If a man is going to love you, he'll love you whether you follow the rule book or not. Women don't get that either."

And women, he adds, "are a lot more interested in relationships anyway than men are. For men, it's number two, after career."

They don't see sex as a means of getting their dependency needs met, and they don't wake up that first morning after automatically planning the wedding. The male pursuit of sex can be as joyless as our pursuit of love and marriage. They use sex as a goal in a macho dating game, as a replacement for touching and closeness, as proof of masculinity, even as a way of avoiding true intimacy. And sometimes winning doesn't feel so good afterward.

One man says: "It can feel like you've jerked off inside another human being. The minutes afterward can be excruciating if you've lied seriously to a woman to bed her. She wants to cuddle. You want to run like hell, from yourself and your own sleazeball mentality as much as her."

The majority of the men in my survey reported that love made sex better for them, including this man, who said: "The closeness makes it not seem like an empty ritual. I find sex with someone I'm not in love with a bit more exciting, but less satisfying."

While love might improve sex for them, it doesn't guarantee monogamous behavior. Approximately half the men who said love made sex better were also not monogamous in committed relationships. For all their ability to make love without loving, however, men seem to have as many emotional problems with breakups as women do.

They may not love "harder," but they do love differently than we do. A woman typically spends a disproportionate amount of time "working" on a new relationship. She is more likely to be the one who sacrifices time with friends, children, career. Who hasn't heard a woman friend say the relationship is keeping her so busy she barely has time to wash her panty hose or buy mascara? Her world shrinks during their building process, his doesn't. But once the two have solidified into a couple, she reaches out to her friends and professional contacts again. And his emotional world shrinks around her.

By the time it's over, he calls her his best friend as well as his lover. She is the emotional center of his life. That relationship may be second to career in his mind, but its absence will leave a gaping hole in his life.

Men may not fall in love every time they have sex, but they do fall.

18 Separation Anxiety

••

"For three months after my divorce, I had problems getting an erection. I forced myself to get right out there—the old 'get back on the horse after you've been thrown' theory—and circulate. More than once I found myself in bed with someone I didn't know well with both of us trying to raise my cock above the half-mast point."

—A forty-seven-year-old painter

A common belief among women is that men have more trouble with breakups than we do. This is probably not true. Rather, each sex has its emotional home remedies for the broken heart, and ours are more efficacious than his. Men handle the situation differently than we do. We cry to all our friends; they hold it inside. While we may not always do so, we believe we *should* give ourselves time to grieve before starting another sexual relationship. They think a real man should "get out there" as soon as possible, like the day after she leaves.

The problems facing newly single men and women are also different. In a divorce, women usually get the kids and a reduced standard of living; men, the child-support payments and a better chance of marrying someone younger and doing it all over again. Following any breakup, women get advice and support from friends; men, invitations to dinners where a single woman is seated next to him. The one piece of advice he gets from his buddies is: Keep busy.

The social system encourages women to express our grief and men to hide theirs. It also nourishes that most difficult man, the newly single man, whom the conventional wisdom has warned us against since we were eighteen. For some period of time following the split—a matter of weeks to years, depending on the man—he's lethal. The system doesn't force him to deal with his emotions, so they may fester for a period long beyond what we would consider excessive in ourselves. He's either out to prove his manhood or to avenge himself on the female sex. Or it's not really over inside his libido.

The questions men ask about love and sex include:

Why am I not enjoying sex as much as I thought I would now that I'm free again?

"Maybe I got so much pleasure in fucking around while I was married because I was cheating. Since we split, sex has been flat. I have no trouble getting women. But sometimes I can't sustain an erection. And sometimes I can't come. It takes more from them to get me off. The only sure thing is anal sex, which is hard to get a woman to do the first time you're together. Is this a normal situation, and how long will it last? Could it be delayed guilt from the way I treated my wife?" writes a thirty-three-year-old Californian.

Men are often surprised to discover the state of their emotional health has some impact on their sexuality. A woman would know the sex is "flat" because she really isn't ready to have sex yet. A man, on the other hand, believes he should always be ready to have sex—and, when he isn't, fears something is wrong with him.

Approximately one third of the men I surveyed reported experiencing sexual difficulties following a breakup—from the inability to achieve or sustain an erection to postcoital depression or vague feelings of discontent. But rarely did they pay attention to the wisdom of the penis.

One man who did writes: "I have finally learned to abstain for a while following a breakup. For at least a month, and maybe more depending on how long I've been with a woman, I'm not interested in sex. I don't even masturbate. Back when I did force myself to have sex anyway, I ended up embarrassing myself and the woman by my failure to perform. Once I started crying. It scared the hell out of the woman. I can't blame her. She hardly knew me."

More typical of the male experience is this: "I might not have performed up to my own standards either after my divorce or the split with my live-in lover, but I performed. I think it's important to keep in the game. I believe in the 'use it or lose it' school of thought. Sure, I was feeling some pain both times, and that may have kept me from enjoying sex to the utmost. On the other hand, sex at less than the utmost is better than no sex at all."

Like many men, this letter writer probably was using sex as a means of avoiding pain—and intimacy. The newly single man isn't looking for another strong emotional connection when he seduces a woman. On the contrary, he is using instant sex to avoid getting to know her on any other level. Some men admit this.

"I've gone directly into a sexual relationship with a new woman following every breakup in my life since I was seventeen," writes a Nashville entertainment lawyer. "I used those women. Whenever I got hurt by a woman, I took all my bad feelings and fucked them right into the next available woman. I don't mean I did that on purpose. It's just what I did, without thinking. In each case, when I was better, I moved on. That's why you should tell women not to get involved with some bastard fresh from divorce court. He's looking for a place to shoot his load—load of grief, that is. Once he does, he's outta there."

If you're looking for a lasting relationship, you should probably avoid the newly single man. With few exceptions, he's a transitional man. When he stops feeling bad, he'll still link you in his mind with that bad period. He may also feel some embarrassment about what he perceived to be his emotional weakness, and perhaps his less-than-perfect sexual performance.

"When a man feels embarrassed about the way he fucked, he dumps the woman," a northeastern businessman writes. "He can't stand to face her again. Hell, yes, it's shitty and cowardly. Men can be cowardly shits."

Sometimes his problem isn't sexual. He may be very good at sex, but unable to trust any woman with his feelings. And he may, or may not, perceive the distrust as *his* problem.

"I've had absolutely no problems performing, but I haven't met a woman I can trust since my divorce three years ago," writes a forty-year-old entrepreneur. "Women want to fuck you dry, physically, financially, and emotionally. If you confide in them, they only use your weaknesses against you. They want too much. Even the women who only want sex want the best sex they ever had every night."

This is an angry man, and you are kidding yourself if you think the love of a good woman will make him better.

Perhaps he would have been forced to come to terms with his bitterness about his divorce if his penis had failed him on occasion. Men can and do use sex to block feelings they don't want to experience and thoughts they don't want to have. And some men can effectively employ the blocking mechanism for years. They can't seem to let go of the past. Nearly a quarter of the men I surveyed reported having great difficulty at least once in their lives in letting go of a woman who had ended the relationship. Several said it took them more than three years. They ask:

Is it abnormal to fantasize an old love while you're fucking someone new?

"Sometimes I think I am sexually addicted to my ex-wife. It's over, and I know it is. But when I bury my nose in a cunt, it's hers I'm smelling. I taste her no matter who I'm eating out. I kiss her, touch her, fuck her. Am I obsessed?" writes a thirty-seven-year-old, divorced for four months.

Vivid sexual fantasies of the former lover may seem like an "obsession" to the afflicted male. If he'd given himself time alone before becoming sexual with a partner again, he might have used the fantasies in masturbation and been able to recognize them for what they are: part of the emotional recovery phase. But men often do not permit themselves the luxury of a slow recovery.

"I once had a terrible time getting over a woman because the sex was so good between us," says a twenty-six-year-old. "I kept calling her to talk until she started hanging up on me. That cured me of calling, but not of fantasizing about her. I fucked women who looked as much like her as possible, and in my mind, she was the one I was always fucking. It finally wore off after five or six months. I began noticing that women who didn't look like her were pretty sexy, too."

Another man, who also rushed into sex though he was "obsessed" with his past lover, says he did so to avoid excessive masturbation.

"I was whacking off four or five times a day, always to memories of her. I had her every which way and then some. It got to the point where I scared myself after a few weeks. So I started going to clubs and picking up women. I still had fantasies of her while I fucked them. At least I wasn't wearing my cock out that way. I had to spend most of the evening getting them into bed."

Few women would want to play the role of surrogate body for the fantasized love object—if they knew they were. Women don't know, because these men lavish attention on them and lie shamelessly. They may be the most ardent suitors. Here is what several told me about their seduction tactics, following a bad breakup:

"Anything is fair. I want to get laid, bad. I'll say anything, do anything, to get a piece of pussy. It's gonna take a lot of pussy to get that woman out of my head."

"After my divorce, women were pretty much interchangeable cunts. I don't say this with pride. It had never been my attitude before. For six months I was a rutting pig—with a silver tongue. I said anything they wanted to hear, including, 'Oh, baby, I love you.' I didn't care what I said. It seemed the end justified the means."

"I was married for ten years. I am Latino, and she cheated on me while I had been true to her. You cannot know unless you are a Latino man what this does to your ego. For two years, I nursed my desire for her and went after other women with a vengeance. I sent more flowers, told more lies than I ever thought possible."

"She was a redhead, and she dumped me. I went after every sexy redhead I saw. I told them I loved them, I wanted them. I even promised to marry one of them on the second date. Well, if she was silly enough to believe it . . ."

If you want a powerful sexual experience, you can probably have it with these men. But don't take it personally. It's sex, not love.

How to Recognize the Emotionally Wounded Man

- He moves too fast. He is too determined to have you. And he's talking love and marriage, those words of balm to single women's hearts, on the second or third date.

- He *hates* his ex. She is a greedy bitch who took something from him.
- He's a liar. You catch him in small lies and wonder why he bothered.
- He abruptly pulls away from you after sex, either emotionally or physically or both.

19 Jealous Lovers

••

"Jealousy is a funny thing. If I'm really jealous of a woman, it can make me hotter for her than ever. But if she's trying to make me jealous with another man, it backfires. I find myself laughing at her because she's a little pathetic in her way of expressing her need. And her need for me is stronger then than mine for her."

—A Southerner

Women frequently advise friends to "make him jealous" when a man has grown complacent and/or has failed to "make a commitment" within a reasonable period of time. We take this position because we assume jealousy has the same effect on them that it has on us: renewing one's interest in the love object. Women meet erotic competition with the complete make-over and a new garter belt. We "fight" for him. If we discover he's slept with her in spite of the heroic battle we've waged, we may be too hurt and angry to have sex with him. We don't feel sexy; we feel hurt.

Men are less inclined to engage in a battle of roses for the lady's affections than they are to be aroused by the thought of another man's having carnal knowledge of her. (No matter how many times you've seen it happen in romantic comedies, real men rarely match each other a dozen roses for a dozen roses to win a woman's hand.) A real rival will probably inspire him to physical passion, because men are competitive. But a contrived rivalry might leave him laughing—at you.

Only 10 percent of the men I surveyed said they had ever been moved by jealousy to intensify a relationship. Most took a rather haughty stand regarding the supposed power of the green-eyed monster over them. They ask:

Why do women make such an effort to get you jealous?

"Jealousy is insecurity, and I would never put myself in the category. I am not concerned if the women I see are seeing other men. So what?" writes a thirty-five-year-old northeasterner.

An astonishing number of men, perhaps the majority, really do not care about sexual exclusivity in their relationships unless they are married or living with a woman. Back in high school, they tumbled to the girls' efforts to manipulate them into "going steady" by making them jealous. It doesn't work anymore—or at least, not most of the time.

A Southern construction workers says: "One of the dumbest, most easy-to-see-through female ploys is that bit where she tells you she's busy when you ask for Saturday night. This is after you've seen her for six or eight Saturday nights in a row. She's trying to push something by making you think she's got another date. You're supposed to get jealous and ask her to be your woman."

And from another man: "Men are pretty stupid emotionally, but after a lot of years we do catch on to some of the little tricks women use to manipulate us. Pretending there's someone else is older than Cleopatra's black eyeliner. I can predict with reasonable accuracy when a woman's going to do it, usually between three and six months of dating with no commitment."

Men also don't understand why jealousy inspires us to compete by upgrading our appearance. Why, they wonder, do we assume the other woman is prettier? They think competition should raise our sexual temperatures, if anything—not our credit limits from having purchased new clothes.

"I date two women who only recently found out about each other," writes a corporate vice-president. "They have each told me that in time they will expect me to choose one over the other. They've issued time-limit ultimatums, one three months, one four months. Having said that, both women changed their hair color. The brunette is now a blonde. The blonde is now a strawberry blonde. One has a new collection of silk lingerie that rivals a Victoria's Secret shop. The other went for clothes she could wear in public, but they're very sexy clothes. Neither one of them changed the way they fuck. Women are curious. A man in the same position would be fucking for his life."

When a man is truly jealous, he is more likely to show his feelings by making love all night than outdoing his rival in the courtship department.

"I was very jealous of the other man my wife was dating when I first met her," writes a thirty-year-old auto mechanic. "He had more money, and I couldn't have outdone him on restaurants and big nights out if I'd wanted to. I figured if she was the woman for me, I'd win her in the sack, not over a bottle of French wine. When I fucked her, I imagined him with a potbelly and a little dick standing in the corner watching us. I fucked her brains out. She got rid of him."

Some men actually relish having sex with a woman shortly after she's been with another man. Perhaps they feel like they're invading his territory. Over the years, many men have even written to ask me how they could get their wives to have sex with another man so they could enjoy the experience of "buttered buns"—having sex with her right after she's been with another man. They often ask:

How can I convince my wife it's okay to fuck someone else?

"Our mutual friend is very attracted to her, and I think she would like to have him, too. But she denies this. I am very turned on by the idea of the two of them having sex. I would like her to meet him at a hotel, then come home and tell me every detail while I fuck her. She says this is depraved. Is it?" writes a reader.

It's a fairly common fantasy. Many men imagine their wives or lovers having sex with another man. In their scenario, they are more powerful lovers than their rivals. And some do want to take the experience beyond the mind-play stage. While most men wouldn't set up the situation, they do react passionately when they discover their lovers are sexually involved with someone else.

"I caught my wife in bed with another man once," confides a fifty-year-old. "It had quite an impact on my libido. The very day it happened I jumped her bones before his come was dry inside her, and I kept jumping her for weeks afterward. I wanted her ferociously.

I never told her this, but I wouldn't have minded a repeat performance of that scene."

Men who don't stumble upon the lovers in the act frequently do ask their women for the details. This may be their way of owning her affair. Or it may simply be what they say it is: a potent verbal aphrodisiac.

"My wife thinks I'm crazy, but I want to know everything about how her lover is with her," writes a forty-year-old man. "Everything—from how big his cock is in comparison to mine to how long he can last and how he eats her out. She says this is my way of ending her affair, by taking it away from her piece by piece. If it is, I don't know what I'm doing then. I just want to know because it makes me hot. I've been able to have two orgasms on more than one occasion since she started seeing this guy."

Because women don't fully understand how erotic rivalry affects men, we often accuse them of latent homosexuality when they show so much interest in our affairs.

"My lover thinks I'm a secret fag because I'd like to watch her making love with another man," writes a twenty-five-year-old. "I also like to hear what happened when she was in bed with other men. But I don't think that makes me queer. There are some things women don't get about men. This is one of them. You like to think no other man could bring her off like you can. But you'd also like to see one try."

It is indeed a mistake to assume that one jealous heart is the same as another. Green comes in shades of his and hers.

What to Remember About Men and Jealousy

- Don't try to make him jealous to force a commitment.
- Don't assume his interest in the sexual details of another relationship is somehow perverse.
- Do be careful of men who are excessively jealous of you. If the reaction persists beyond the early courtship stage, it may be indicative of a possessive, controlling man.

20 Monogamy, His and Hers

••

"Men have sex whenever they are horny, like you eat when you're hungry. Women (most, not all) think a man should be in love with a woman before they have sex, and that just isn't the case. A man can love his wife and never want to leave her, but prefer having sex with someone else because they are giving him something he doesn't get at home or they are a better lover. This doesn't mean they love their wife less or that they are falling in love with the sex partner."

—A thirty-four-year-old divorced consultant

Possibly this man's former wife didn't agree. But their marriage may have ended for other reasons than his sexual liaisons. The statisticians from Kinsey through Hite keep telling us that as many as 80 percent of husbands do have extramarital affairs. (In recent years, the wives have been closing the gap.) A lot of my reader mail has concerned questions of infidelity. And slightly less than 50 percent of the men I surveyed (who are or had been married) reported having extramarital affairs.

Some men tell their wives. More don't. Many of them get caught anyway. Few marriages qualify as "open"—where spouses give each other permission to have sex outside the marriage. The double standard still exists in judging the importance of an affair. The overwhelming majority of men say their affairs are "meaningless," while they see their wives' affairs as a threat to the marriage.

"Women get involved with their guts as much as their genitals," one man says. "They're looking for emotional involvement when they go outside the marriage. Men are looking for sex."

That's an oversimplification of the motives men and women have for seeking extramarital sex, but it's a belief to which many husbands subscribe. Maybe they want to believe women look for love and romance, not sex, because it's easier to accept themselves as deficient at being romantic than at being sexual. Their own reasons for looking elsewhere include:

"I wanted anal sex and fellatio, which I wasn't getting at home."

"It was usually a spur-of-the-moment thing. One time a neighbor and I had a few drinks together in the afternoon. We went dancing that night and ended up in a hotel room. It was a fun night."

"I don't get enough sex at home."

And that old, oft-repeated fallback excuse, the macho code as justification for extramarital sex: "Men aren't naturally monogamous. We don't need a reason, only an opportunity."

One man said: "I wasn't satisfied with the marriage, with her." And another said: "I think subconsciously I wanted the marriage to end, and I knew she would leave me if I cheated on her. So I did it and left a lot of clues."

Few of these men expressed regret over their affairs. One who did, said, "I don't know if my first wife knew about my affairs or if they affected our marriage, but I'm not taking the risk this time. I feel badly about the mistakes I made the first time and don't want to repeat them."

What men usually ask about extramarital sex is:

How can I keep my wife from finding out about my lover?

"This is my second marriage, and I don't want it to fail. Women seem to have a sixth sense about cheating men. What are the things that give us away? I'm smart enough not to get lipstick on my collar or leave phone numbers on matchbooks. What's the real skinny? How do women figure it out?" writes a forty-three-year-old from Houston.

I think there are women who know and women who choose not to know. The latter group won't figure it out unless he humiliates them with the obvious—i.e., the lipstick-stained collar. The first group will know. He might get by with the occasional spur-of-the-moment liaison, but he won't hide a continuing affair from them.

Relatively few magazine articles are devoted to telling a woman how to know if he's having an affair or not. She doesn't need help in that department. Rather, the majority of articles on infidelity promise secrets to keep him in her bed. The critical question women ask is: How can I keep him faithful? I put it to several men, including those who were most concerned with hiding their infidelities. They said:

"My wife could give me everything I want and at some point I would still be vulnerable to another woman simply because she's different."

"Probably a combination of fulfilling my every sexual fantasy—and then going cold on me for a few weeks. I would never have her figured out. But I said, probably. I'm not sure."

"Anal sex. Let me come in her mouth."

"I would probably be afraid to cheat on a woman too secure to devour all those dumb books on how to keep her man happy at home."

"Eventually, at least for a moment, everyone, man or woman, regards monogamy as the price you pay to maintain something that matters more than anything else in your life. I've cheated with other women, but I won't with this woman, because she makes me feel the cost is a small one in comparison to what I have with her."

"If she would lose the fifty pounds she's gained since I married her and do something about her other problem—locked thighs."

"I wouldn't cheat on a woman I loved if I truly believed I could lose her over it. A lot of women say they'd leave 'if he did such and such.' Ninety percent are bluffing, and you know it. They'll find an excuse for their man no matter what. A few women really mean it. If a woman made me happy most of the time—which is all you can ask of anyone—and made me believe she'd walk if I gave her reason, I wouldn't give her reason."

Their feelings about their lovers ranged from "purely sexual" to "love." Yet few men said their affairs led directly to divorce. And when they did, the lover hardly ever became the second wife.

This man's story is typical: "I had an affair after twenty-two years of a faithful, loving, but sexually unsatisfying marriage. My affair was with a married lady fifteen years younger than myself. She got divorced and I went a little cuckoo. She was in my every thought.

I was possessed for about a year and a half. But I didn't want to leave my wife for her. Finally I found another married lady and am living happily ever after. Sorry, but true."

The "other woman" gets the man more often in the movies than in real life. Ironically, the wife seems to take her more seriously than the husband generally does. Most of the advice she receives tells her to appease him, sexually and otherwise, and then to give him the ultimatum, her or me. But what men said to me is: Yes, we want rich, full sex lives, but that alone won't keep us from straying. A self-respecting woman who absolutely won't put up with it, might.

Women's affairs also concern men, but not yet as much as theirs do us. The question they most often ask is:

Why is she having an affair with another man?

"It's not like she can't get enough sex at home. I usually want it more than she does. She swears he doesn't have a bigger cock than I do or do anything differently in bed than I do. Then why would she be with him? What are women looking for if they aren't looking for better sex?" writes a thirty-two-year-old.

A woman sees a man's affair as a rejection of her physical self. She imagines the other woman as younger, thinner, prettier, and she is sure her fat thighs have driven him into someone else's bed. A man may see a woman's affair as a rejection of him sexually. He is convinced the other man has a larger penis or is able to maintain an erection longer than he is or has the secret to giving her multiple orgasms.

Even men who are not threatened by their wives' sexual involvements become concerned if those relationships escalate to the affair stage.

"My wife has had the occasional fling while traveling on business," writes a forty-five-year-old man. "I don't see that as any different from similar experiences of mine. She has told me about them, and we have both found our little infidelities have added zest to our sex life. Recently she started seeing a man who works in her office. This is different. She meets him once a week on a regular basis. I don't think she would be doing this if she weren't getting something from him she isn't getting at home. At first it made me jealous. Now it's making me angry."

Many other men saw a difference between the fantasized, or sometimes real, sex their partners had with other men and shared with them through exchanges of confidence and the full-blown affair, a union of two lovers who share secrets. It is most likely the wives, they report, who decide to leave a marriage because of these affairs. Breaking her confidence with her lover may be seen as a way of weakening that bond in favor of the marital tie.

"Sexual secrets, not just sex, can destroy a relationship," says a husband of fifteen years. "My wife has a much greater sex drive than I do, and I have come to accept that and let her seek gratification elsewhere, as long as she doesn't hide anything from me. I want to know everything she does with other men. For a while she was cheating on me behind my back, and that almost broke us up. Now I know who her partners are and what they do with her."

And from another man: "I was thirty when we married and she was twenty-three. She grew up in Britain in a rural area. . . . I had several sex partners before marriage and she had few. She wondered about what she may have missed in her early years, and most important, her sexual drive was much stronger than mine. She wanted sexual intercourse more often than I was ready for it, and it was a strong desire on her part. . . . Once I understood her needs, I agreed that she could have sex with certain other men after we discussed it. This is a very good arrangement."

This is not a situation most would find comfortable. But many men have written to tell me they've "forgiven" or "understood" their wives' affairs once the details were shared with them. The knowledge perhaps restores some of the control they felt was lost.

Control is part of the hidden agenda in "swinging" relationships, which still do exist in America. A minority of couples participate in these structured group alliances, which meld monogamy and cheating. Over the years some men have written to ask:

How can I get my wife to swing?

"We are good friends with two other couples, and the sexual vibes between the six of us are strong. At one time or another every one of us has made a

teasing reference to group sex or swinging. I know the men are ready, and the women wouldn't take much priming. If my wife and I initiated something, the other four would fall out of their clothes, ten seconds flat. How do I persuade her to take the plunge?" writes a reader.

I advise any man who wants his wife to grant a sexual wish to sound her out in conversation, and unless she is horrified or angered by the subject, *ask*. Men are no different from women in their hope that clever manipulative tactics will get them what they want from the opposite sex. Few people try the direct approach first.

My survey questionnaire fell into the hands of a longtime swinger, who asked if he could make copies and distribute it to other swingers. (Many respondents did copy and send the questionnaire to friends, which probably accounts for my higher-than-normal return rate.) Twenty-five swingers did participate. Of that group, twenty indicated they had initiated the swinging, not their wives. The other five didn't say. Based on this and other observations, I think swinging appeals more to the husband than to the wife, because it sets up open liaisons based solely or largely on sex. No secrets. No romance.

One man explains the process: "We don't belong to a regular group, though some people do. We meet couples through ads in swinging publications. The decision to do it this way rather than maintaining a close group tie was my wife's. She didn't want the threat of emotional involvement, which she thought could happen if we fucked the same people all the time. Of course, we ask to see medical proof of negative AIDS testing, which we also provide."

Another explains his motives: "I convinced my wife to swing by explaining to her that I was going after more sex, with her or without her. I have a high sex drive, a strong need for variety. I love my wife very much. And I want to stay faithful to her, in the sense of being honest with her and not leaving her out of my other sex life. It has not worked perfectly. She is prone to getting jealous sometimes anyway. But it works better than me cruising chicks on my own would work for her."

No one has written to tell me his wife got him involved in swinging, though I'm sure such situations must exist. I've also had few letters from men who say either they or their wives became emotionally involved with a sex partner. But this man did:

"I fell in love with, and eventually married, a woman I met through an upper-crust swingers' group in Boston in the late Seventies. We both realized we didn't belong in that situation. To tell you the truth, I think a lot of the people who tried it when swinging was in its heyday didn't belong. Couples went off into bedrooms or dark corners and came back saying how great it had been. A lot of that was locker-room talk. It was unusual only in that you rarely get that kind of talk from a mixed crowd. I faked more than one boffo climax as a swinger. There was enough flavored lubricants in that crowd to open a juice shop."

If monogamy has its pitfalls, so do the alternatives.

What You Can Do About His Infidelities

- Pretend they don't exist.
- Issue an ultimatum, but only if you intend to follow through.
- Tell him you know, but have chosen, for now, to overlook them.

And What You Probably Can't Do

- Lure him back to monogamy with a new look.

Part Six

SECRET FEARS AND HIDDEN OBSESSIONS

No, Vernon, There Is No Penis Enlarger

•••

"Is there any way of enlarging a small penis? Mine is very short, and I think I am unable to satisfy a woman with it. This makes me very unhappy. Do those devices to increase length work, and if so, do they have side effects?"
                                                              —A reader

The tiny ads in the cheap-rate section at the back of our magazines tout "bust expanders," creams, lotions, and an exercising gadget that looks like a large rubber band. The ads in the backs of men's magazines promise that the Vacuum Enlarger, a wicked little suction machine, can actually make the penis grow. ("Some men might still believe that it's not the size of the sword, but the swordsmanship . . . but wouldn't you rather go into a battle with a lance than a dagger?") Many women assume male and female size obsessions are equivalent, like the space taken up by sleazy ads for rip-off products. They are wrong. We have no single body part concern that correlates to their male fixation: penis size.

Men have penis envy. Women don't. The average penis is three inches flaccid and six inches when fully erect. The smaller the penis, the more it grows in erection, so that most erections are about the same size. Men absolutely do not believe this. They are sure they are smaller than the average man, whom they take to be the man photographed in erotic layouts. (Those organs may be somewhat larger than average, but they are also miraculously expanded by a photographic technique known as "shooting up from under.")

The number-one question men have asked me over the years is: How important is penis size to women?

No matter how many times we tell them size doesn't matter,

they do not believe us. (And a few women do tell them it matters. I've received letters from men who say their partners told them they were too small to "give" her orgasms!) About 75 percent of the men in my survey said penis size was important to them and 60 percent said it was to women. Their comments included:

"I am small, but thank God I erect to seven and a half inches. Also I curve. Girls really like this."

"Being about average, I don't think it's important at all. If I had a small penis, I would think it was important."

"I think women will accept a size deficiency if you get really hard. If you're small and not that hard, you are in a bad way."

"It's the measure of my life."

"Probably not as important to women as men think. Probably."

"I feel size is more important to women than the surveys report. Women think it is not nice to say they want a big one. Truth is, they're attracted to a man with a nice bulge in his pants."

Everyone who studies male sexuality is confronted with the penis-size question. While the majority of men think they are too small, a sizable minority (about 25 percent of the men who've written to my columns and 20 percent of the survey respondents) swear they are large to enormous. According to Kinsey, less than 2 percent of men are large, or greater than six inches when flaccid. White men truly believe black men are much bigger than they are. According to Kinsey again, black men are less than one fourth of an inch larger than white men on the average.

Shere Hite found the male emphasis on penis size "closely related to the pressure on [them] to be sexually active on a frequent basis." I would take that even further. Sexually, a man believes he *is* his penis.

Consider the enlightened man, who knows the vagina can accommodate itself to any size penis and understands female orgasm is largely dependent on clitoral stimulation. Though he is well aware the clitoris is not located inside the vagina, this man will still insist a well-endowed man is more likely to satisfy his partner than a lesser endowed man is.

Men are erotic visualists. They are convinced the sight of a large and beautiful male organ excites a woman. Their eye—penis connection is strong, and they assume we, too, have a close link between sight and erotic arousal. The strength of that connection for them (and not us) may also explain why so many male obsessions are expressed in terms of body parts and objects and why there are no correlating female obsessions. Fetishists are always men.

If women sometimes inhabit the Victorian attics of the sexual house where we lie faint with romantic fantasies and the vapors brought on by desire, men flee to the dark closets, where the darker expressions of their sexuality can be hidden from us. Because of the way their brains are made, men tend to have more visual perversions, or needs that deviate from the norm than we do. And because sex is more dependent on male arousal than female, they tend to act out their perversions while we may only fantasize about ours.

Everyone has a sexual secret. I believe the most common male secret is that he secretly masturbates when he could have sex with his partner. But some men have other secrets: the fear of being gay, dependence on the presence of a fetish for erection and ejaculation, deep need for sexual practices that involve dominance and submission and humiliation.

They are the secret needs of the penis, and sometimes the needs are so strong they must be brought from the closet into the light where he can see them. The penis is more than his primary sexual organ. It is the measure of the man himself. If it were any less, his chief sexual concern would not be the question of penis size.

21 Am I Gay?

● ●

"My wife doesn't understand why men don't peek at other men's cocks at the urinal. Women check out other women in the shower room at the club. She doesn't understand men are scared to death another guy will think they're gay if they look. Or worse, they'll think they're gay themselves, every straight man's worst fear."

—A New Yorker

Men are the homophobic sex. While everyone has some homosexual sex fantasies, men seem to worry more about them than women do. Men also fear that gestures of physical affection toward other men might be misinterpreted as sexual advances, so they seldom make them. They don't size each other up in the locker room the way women do after an aerobics class. We are frankly curious about each other. They are afraid to be. Someone might think they are gay.

The use of the term "latent homosexuality" by everyone from therapists to spurned women has helped shore up the macho code. If a real man is always ready for sex, always rock hard, always able to last all night, and always able to satisfy his woman, then it follows that a man who isn't *always* isn't a real man. He might be gay. (Yes, that definition makes every man a target of suspicion at one time or another.) To admit tender feelings for a male friend or lack of desire for an attractive woman opens the door a little wider.

Men believe they have to be very careful. Their eyes or hands or thoughts shouldn't stray to other men's bodies. But they shouldn't pass an attractive woman without wanting to touch her. They are constantly monitoring their responses, checking for the hidden indicators of "latent homosexuality." Over the years, many men have written to ask:

Am I gay?

"When I was thirteen I had a homosexual experience with a group of boys. I could never tell anyone about it because of the guilt. Since my divorce last year, I've had trouble performing with other women. One of them asked if I was queer. I am afraid I am secretly gay or bisexual and have been denying my true feelings all these years," writes a reader.

It is possible, of course, that this man has been suppressing a desire for homosexual sex and "denying true feeling," but it's more likely he hasn't. Early homosexual experiences are common, and so, unfortunately, is the terrible guilt men bear for having experienced them. Nor is "trouble performing" unusual for a man who has gone through a divorce or breakup, especially if sexual problems were part of his past relationship.

Barbach, in *The Intimate Male*, says, "Some men had no trouble achieving an erection but had difficulty maintaining it—especially in situations where they felt particularly vulnerable. This was a fairly pervasive problem for men whose relationships had recently broken up and who once again found themselves back on the singles circuit, especially when former sexual relationships had been fraught with difficulties."

We have great sympathy for women who can't respond sexually after a divorce, much less so for men.

"Single men, even divorced men, are open to the charges of women hating and latent homosexuality," writes a Kentucky teacher. "Maybe women just get mad at us if we aren't hooked up with one of them. It's like they look at us and think, No wonder it's so hard finding a husband when guys like you won't get married. You must be a woman-hating fag.

"Women don't know how sensitive we are to the gay label. Secretly every unattached man is worrying it might be true of him, especially if he's going through a sexual low period. The image of the single man is this guy who fucks his brains out. If you're not that guy, you worry what's wrong with you."

Even men who have participated in group sex—and are presumably more sexually free than most of us—often write either asking if they are gay or insisting they're not.

"I had sex with a buddy and his girl," writes a twenty-nine-year-old, "but my buddy and I didn't do anything to each other. It was all her doing us."

And from another man: "I have been involved a couple of times in small group settings, but no gay stuff. A friend and I double-dated and ended up in someone's apartment. We played strip poker, one thing led to another, and we found ourselves all four nude and fucking in the same room, then switching partners. The guys did not touch each other."

Men who have had bisexual experiences are often concerned about their sexuality and/or are afraid to tell women about this side of them. They write letters sharing long stories, then ask, "Does this mean I like men better than women?" or "What would she think about me if she knew?"

"Drinking usually gets my sex drive going into high gear," a northeasterner writes. "The way it started was one night I was in a peep show in Times Square and a young man came into my booth and asked me if he could 'go down' on me. I was shocked but somewhat excited at the thought of what was about to happen. I remember enjoying it immensely, and when the time came, I had a terrific orgasm. It wasn't long after that I discovered 'all-male' movie theaters were even better. In there I participated in male sex marathons. I really enjoyed sex with men because they had no hang-ups about what they wanted to do and what they wanted done to them. You didn't have to ask, you just did it and everyone was happy. I did this when I was single, and even when I was married. I didn't normally find myself attracted to men, but when I was there and sexually excited, anything went. I stopped immediately when I became aware of AIDS and haven't had any kind of experience with men since.

"I don't think I miss it. What do you think?"

For a short time, bisexuality was chic. AIDS changed that. Now women are scrutinizing men for signs of bisexual tendencies, and men know we are. They ask:

What are the criteria for judging bisexuality?

"I've had a few dates with a woman—no sex yet—who told me I have

all the 'markings' of a gay or bi man. She was spewing facts like crazy. According to her magazines, 80 percent of gay men have had sex with a woman this year without telling her they're gay. And some professional fields are dominated by gay or bisexual men. She mentioned my field, public relations, but then again, she mentioned so many jobs, she covered just about every guy I know. What else makes her suspect me? Am I sending out hidden bi signals? I swear, I'm straight," writes a thirty-one-year-old PR executive.

I have read some articles in women's magazines that make searching for signs of bisexual behavior sound like the modern version of witch-hunting. Obviously, some men do hide bisexual behavior from their female partners, and some men do hate women. But the climate created by AIDS fear and anger at men for not being everyone we want them to be nurtures the macho code and punishes any man who might be slightly effeminate—or, Goddess forbid, working as a hairdresser. In fact, the article this man cited did condemn the jobs and professions that employ many baby-boom men.

Women would be better advised to delay sex until they know their partners better, trust their instincts, and *always* use condoms than to study his behavior for "signs" of bisexuality.

"It's hard to win these days," one man writes. "If you hold off on pushing for sex, a woman thinks you're gay. Pull out a condom and she starts to cry, saying, 'This means you're seeing someone else, doesn't it?' Personally, I am just as concerned about getting AIDS as women are, maybe more so."

And from another man: "My women friends are obsessed now with how they can tell if a guy might be bisexual. They've asked me if I know the signs. This is just one more example of women focusing on the wrong thing. Instead of admitting sex is a serious proposition for everyone today and taking responsibility for themselves by using condoms, they are trying to put responsibility and blame back on men. They're saying everything would be okay if they didn't have to worry about some of us being secret fags."

Perhaps if women understood how much men secretly fear being gay, we wouldn't add to their concerns by accusing them of homosexual or bisexual behavior on such "proof" as his failure to perform sexually or his choice of nursing as a profession.

A male nurse from Chicago writes: "You can't imagine the pressure I get because of my career. I work on a children's AIDS ward, and I know in my heart and gut I'm doing the most important work I could be doing right now. I also know I'm a pure 100-percent heterosexual man. It's lucky I have confidence in myself because many women don't even want to go out with me as soon as they hear I'm a nurse. They tell me to my face, 'You must be gay.' Whatever happened to all those women who wanted more sensitive men?"

Good question. A lot of men have asked it lately, too.

One Almost Foolproof Method for Determining His Sexual Tendencies

• Introduce him to your gay friends. If he is, they'll probably know.

22 Sexual Footmen

••

"It started because I liked the feel of women's silk panties rubbing over the head of my cock. I masturbated that way when I was a teenager, using my mother's panties from the laundry hamper. Later on, I started wearing silk panties under my clothes at home. I can't have sex with a woman unless she's wearing panties at the time. The ones with thin crotches are preferable to the crotchless kind. Sometimes I can come from just holding a pair of used silk panties against my face and breathing hard."

—A northeastern physician

He has a lingerie fetish—or to be more exact, a fetish for silk panties, worn and scented by a woman's body. A fetish may be a body part—the most common being, feet—or an item of clothing—the most common being worn panties. Some men have a fondness for certain body parts or items of female clothing, but their liking for them does not make them fetishists. The man above is not able to reach orgasm without the presence of "used" silk panties. When a need for the object is carried to this extreme degree, the object has become a fetish. Arousal and ejaculation depend on it.

While many desire or crave the presence of certain erotic elements in lovemaking, few men are true fetishists. The experts generally agree the fetish has developed to allow these men some means of expressing a sexuality that has been severely repressed, either by family or religious training or early sexual abuse. (Male children are also often victims of abuse.) Because their needs are different from those we define as "normal," fetishists can frighten women, and they know it. The question they've most often asked me is:

How can I get her to let me worship her feet?

"I love the female foot. When I see a shapely female foot encased in sexy

high heels—the higher, the better—I get a hard-on. If the foot belongs to an attractive lady I'd like to be with, I want to throw myself on the ground and begin worshiping her feet. I want to remove her stockings and shoes and bathe and cream her feet and polish her toenails. And when they are perfect, I want to suck each toe and lick the instep until I make her shiver with joy. But why are so many women turned off to the idea of foot worship?" writes a reader.

I advise foot fetishists to begin their adoration of the chosen female at a higher level and work down. While the foot may be his object of desire, it is not often the body part a woman considers her most erotic. But having one's toes sucked and instep licked can be a pleasantly sensual experience, especially if it's preceded by kissing, licking, and sucking of the rest of the body. The man who goes straight for the feet will surely make his partner nervous.

Fetishists who have been less than subtle report devastating experiences.

"Once, many years ago, I made the mistake of cutting straight from kissing her mouth to her feet," writes a thirty-nine-year-old. "She giggled at first, saying I was tickling her. Then she was embarrassed and asked me to stop because her feet weren't clean. But, of course, they were. Finally she jerked her foot out of my mouth and started yelling that I was a pervert. Unfortunately, I had already come while sucking her toes. I learned to be more circumspect. Sometimes I can come if I'm in a position to see her feet; '69' works best, if she doesn't mind me coming in her mouth, or if I can feel her feet wrapped securely around my neck."

Some fetishists work out carefully planned sex scenarios, worthy of erotic sitcoms, so the fetish need can be satisfied without the woman's knowing it has been.

"I cannot reach orgasm unless I am fucking a woman who is wearing high heels," writes a forty-two-year-old. "Sometimes I can convince a woman to wear her heels to bed. I don't ask unless I know her well. In the beginning of a relationship, I may have to fake coming several times. Then she will feel comfortable enough with me to wear the shoes to bed. Or even better, I can merely remove her panties and make love to her fully clothed. A woman finds it sexy if she thinks you're so overcome by passion you have to fuck her shortly after getting in the door."

A lingerie fetish seems like a simple obsession by comparison. Men who require the presence of certain kinds of lingerie are luckier than the foot worshiper. Lingerie is considered an acceptable form of arousal to most of us, and many women don't mind making love in garter belts and stockings or lace teddies because they hide love handles and other fleshy parts. The acceptability of this obsession can mask its true character, even to the man.

"I didn't realize I had grown totally dependent on black garter belts and stockings until I met a woman who wouldn't wear them," writes a thirty-three-year-old. "I had made an erotic game of it with past partners, presenting them with expensive lace garter belts and silk stockings and dressing them in my gifts as part of foreplay. On subsequent occasions if they chose not to wear these things, I could still come by fantasizing them as they had looked. When I met a woman who wouldn't play at all, I tried fantasy, but it didn't work. And since then, fantasy hasn't worked."

Other men have told me their dependence on the fetish seemed to develop gradually over time. They moved from using it in fantasy to needing its actual presence for orgasm, and finally for arousal. As young men, their arousal occurred more easily. They were erotic specialists, but not extreme specialists. Beyond thirty, thirty-five, or forty, they were no longer aroused without the fetish.

"I feel like an old pervert now," admits a man whose fetish is long, dark hair. "When my girlfriend cut her hair, I was impotent. I convinced her to wear a wig, but she hates wearing it. By cutting off her hair, she brought this out in the open, where neither one of us is comfortable with it."

A few men report the drive to meet their fetish needs has led them into compromising positions. A question I've had many times is:

How can I collect women's soiled panties without getting caught?

"I have a fetish for women's panties, preferably silk ones edged in lace,

but they must have been recently worn. I like to wear them for a while and feel my cock throbbing against the place where her pussy has creamed. Then I take them off and use them to masturbate. Sometimes I come in them. Or sometimes I save them to sniff and use again later. The problem is obviously one of supply. Recently I was caught in the laundry basket at a friend's apartment. It was embarrassing, to say the least. Is there a place where a man can buy previously worn panties?" writes a reader.

Not that I think the idea is inconceivable, but I don't know of a used-panty fulfillment center. Products and publications aimed at highly specialized sex markets exist in abundance. There are spanking newsletters and mail-order companies that handle nothing but spanking "instruments." There are magazines devoted solely to pictures of large breasts and others dedicated to feet. An underground industry services most of men's fetishes, but some needs can't be easily met. Used panties is one of them.

Still, I don't recommend stealing from laundry hampers. Perhaps a frank talk with a female friend who would trade old panties for new? A few men have written to tell me they worked out such an arrangement. Others "borrow" from their girlfriends.

"My girlfriend doesn't know I masturbate with her soiled panties," writes a California lawyer. "But I think she might be getting suspicious. She teases me about losing a lot of panties at my place. Sometimes she asks me to model her panties for her, and I do. So maybe she thinks I'm wearing them, not jerking off in them. Should I tell her, or would it turn her stomach?"

Fetishists usually keep their secret as long as possible. If they are hurt by suppressing the truth, they are also wounded by the accusations and rejection that can follow sexual honesty.

"Women seem to think that if you have one perversion, you have them all," writes an East Coast foot fetishist. "You tell them how you feel about feet and they say they can't trust you with their children because you might molest them. It's happened to me. I don't blame the women entirely. If you keep something hidden, you're treating it like it's a sickness."

Fetishism is an area of male sexuality not readily accessible to women. This is something we "don't get" about men. If you care about a man who has a fetish, get professional help in handling your feelings and attitudes.

What to Remember About a Fetishist

- He isn't violent or dangerous.
- He has two secrets, causing him pain: the fetish and cruelty in his childhood.
- Telling you was harder than anything he's ever done.
- The fetish is his visual link to his own sexuality. If he gives it up, without professional help, he is left with no means of touching his sexuality, no way to become aroused or ejaculate.

23 Sexual Slaves

••

"I am a normal person. I lead a normal life, with the exception that it is more privileged than most. One afternoon a week I visit a dominatrix. She makes me strip and kneel before her naked to lick her boots. Sometimes she urinates on me. Sometimes she makes me hold a difficult position. It always ends with a caning across my bare ass. I always come."

—A corporate executive, age forty

A few men take the fantasies common to many and make them real. Sex for these men is linked, often inextricably, to humiliation, punishment, and pain. Many people label their behavior "degenerate" or "perverse." In the psychiatric and biomedical communities their sexual perversions are called "paraphilias."

Women who have perversions are almost entirely masochists. Men have a wider range of paraphiliac expression. They may be masochists or sadists, cross-dressers or extreme fetishists. Male paraphilias are visually oriented: the extensive paraphenalia used in bondage and S&M, the clothing and makeup a cross-dresser wears, the sight of a woman as either dominatrix or abject sexual slave. Man's strong visual orientation is only one reason his range of dark sexual expression is greater than woman's. According to the experts, at the heart of all perverse sex practices is the inability to form a romantic love bond. Because of their ability to separate sex and love, men are more likely to be unable to bring the two together than women are.

Dr. John Money, the foremost researcher on the origins of paraphilia, says, "The basic theorem of all the paraphilias is that probably from the time of childhood sexual rehearsal play, lust gets separated from love. Anything below the belt is lust and punishable, and love, affection, and poetry go above the belt with kissing."

Money has *not* found a causal connection between pornography and aberrant sexual practices. Rather, he believes pornography has become the scapegoat for behavior the general public can't understand or condone. Even before the revelation that several prominent right-wing religious leaders had been involved in steamy sex scandals, Money was equating super-righteous crusading with kinkiness.

"When I see somebody who carries self-righteousness to excess," he says, "I just automatically say, 'If I scratch the surface on this one, I'll find the sin under there.' "

Judging from my mail, I believe that the men who submit to the dominatrix's heavy paddle come from repressive and/or excessively religious family backgrounds. They are rigid, driven, overachieving men who find release in painful and humiliating submission. Like anyone else, they are entitled to their sexual pleasure—whether we understand it or not—as long as that pleasure isn't taken from another without consent.

While a few are enslaved, many people have experimented with some forms of bondage and light S&M. (Perhaps this is due in part to the popularization of S&M images in the Eighties, including leather clothing, punk hair and jewelry, domination-and-submission backgrounds for music videos.) Over a third of the respondents in my survey had participated, usually in bondage or spanking. Most had done so from curiosity or a lover's request. The question they most often ask is:

Is it abnormal?

"My girlfriend and I were playing around in bed one day. She slapped me playfully across my bare ass. I slapped her back. One thing led to another and we were making love. She was on top. Suddenly she asked me to slap her again on the buttocks. I did. She said, 'Again. A little harder.' I spanked her in rhythm with our fucking. She really got off on it. Spanking her didn't do anything for me until I saw her rosy red ass. Then I got hot as blazes and we fucked again, harder than the first time. Is there something wrong with us?" writes a reader.

Dr. Ruth calls letters of this type "requests for permission." The writer feels guilty and wants an authority figure to absolve him of his guilt. Some people feel guilty about spending five minutes in the missionary position. They are more likely to write to Dr. Ruth than to the Superlady of Sex. At *Forum* and *Penthouse Letters*, I received permission requests that indicated, for the most part, a familiarity and comfort with basic sex. (I did, however, get a lot of mail from married men who confessed they masturbated "behind her back" and wondered if that was wrong.) Many wanted someone to tell them it wasn't "abnormal" to experiment with some of the kinkier forms of sex.

Not once did a man write to say he wanted to rape or inflict undesired pain upon a woman. Men like that don't consult sex-advice columnists for their opinion. But men whose desires run a little outside the publicly drawn sexual lines often do need reassurance from someone.

"When I was twenty, I had an affair with a married woman of thirty-eight," writes a Midwesterner. "She loved to be spanked while I stimulated her clit with my hand. I got to enjoy this practice. To this day I get an instant erection spanking a woman. Is this a conditioned response? Should I be concerned?"

And from another man: "I've gotten into some kinky stuff with my girlfriend. We take turns tying each other up. The bound person is sometimes blindfolded, too. The person in charge teases the other sexually by stimulating, then stopping, and so on. The point is to get her (or me) as hot as possible before letting her (or me) come. Sometimes, too, she likes me to strap her lightly with my belt on the insides of her thighs. Is this going to lead us into heavier stuff?"

Masochists do outnumber sadists. The letters I've received from men whose partners initiated the spanking exceeded those from men who wanted advice on how to convince a woman to submit to the palm or hairbrush. And there were far more letters—at least four to one—from men who describe themselves as "slaves" than from those who play the "master" role.

This is a fairly typical letter from a slave who lives with his mistress: "On discipline day, my mistress makes me wear a black leather collar attached to a leash, black leather wrist and ankle bands with attachments for binding me together, weighted nipple clamps, and a cock ring [a device that makes erection painful]. I am forced to do her bidding without speaking. If I displease her, she whacks me with a riding crop. Though she repeatedly stimulates me and I am expected to give her many orgasms orally, I am not allowed to come all day. If I do, she makes me lick up my own come. At the end of the day, I am sore and exhausted but too keyed up to sleep. I lie awake most of the night, my cock throbbing in agony and anticipation, waiting for morning when I can fuck her."

A smaller group of men enjoy a practice known as "golden showers" or sometimes "water sports," which involves urination.

"I like a woman to stand astride me and piss on me," says a twenty-nine-year-old businessman. "If she can make it last awhile, by starting and stopping her urine, I can come this way."

And another says: "It's the ultimate form of degradation, to use another person as your toilet. Sometimes I need that. I need to grovel in that, to revel in the piss, shit, and slime of humanity."

Whatever his "perversion," a man is rarely confident about sharing it with the woman he loves. Many men have hidden their dark desires from their wives for years. They pay prostitutes or dominatrixes to indulge the passions they consider too "dirty" for her. But other men want to come out of their particular closets, many after years, even decades, of hiding. They write:

How can I tell her?

"I am a cross-dresser, but my fiancée does not know. I started dressing in women's clothes when I was a little kid. My father caught me once parading around the house in my mother's heels, dress, and makeup, and he whaled the tar out of me. He said, 'That will teach you a lesson, and it did. I learned to hide. I have two trunks of clothes, everything from padded bras and girdles to high-heeled shoes. I have wigs and a makeup case. And I long to show this side of me to the woman I love, but I am afraid she will reject me. How should I go about letting her know?" writes a thirty-four-year-old businessman.

A minority of men cross-dress. Some are content merely to wear the clothing and makeup at home. Others go out dressed as women. A few can only make love wearing silky lingerie and lipstick and eye shadow. The man above has been able to hide his "perversion" from his partner because he isn't totally dependent on it for sexual arousal or orgasm. She probably has no idea that he cross-dresses. If there were hints, she didn't pick them up.

He is right in assuming she will be, at the least, not happy. I recommend getting professional help in sharing that kind of information. Several men have written to tell me they did get counseling. In some cases, it helped the woman accept this other side; in others, it helped him cope with her rejection.

"I did it the wrong way," a midwesterner writes. "I unlocked the wardrobe and showed her my clothes. She freaked. Worse, she told all her friends; and I live in a small town. I guess I don't blame her. If I'd prepared her better, maybe she could have, if not accepted, at least understood."

It is, however, difficult for women to understand why a man wants to dress like a woman. She assumes he must want to have sex with men, and that isn't the case. Cross-dressers are usually heterosexual men. They explain their predilections by saying:

"It started as a joke when I was in college. A group of girls held me down in the dorm and put makeup all over my face. I liked it."

"I love the sensual feel of women's clothing, particularly underthings. The contrast of silk and lace with my coarse hairy body excites me."

"Wearing women's lingerie makes me feel like I am somehow androgynous, but when I fuck, I want to fuck a woman."

"It feels good, sensual, dangerous, exciting. I know when I go out dressed as a woman that I am taking my life in my hands. Some guy could kill me. It gets my adrenaline up."

"My first successful masturbation occurred in a woman's closet where I had found a girdle that I put on. The pressure of the garment caused an ejaculation with no other stimulation. In the following years, most of my erotic stimulation came from lingerie and foundation ads. Even today I occasionally reach an ejaculation simply by wearing a garter belt, panties, and hose. I do not otherwise have a feminine persona. I have found that women neither understand nor appreciate this."

And a psychologist who is a cross-dresser says: "Maybe if men were allowed to exhibit our feminine and submissive side, we wouldn't have the fierce need to repress it—and the corresponding urge to surrender to it. That for me is what cross-dressing is all about, the terrible push and pull of the male and female inside me. But I don't mean that to be a scientific explanation. It's just how it is for me."

Cross-dressing may be difficult for us to understand because there is no comparable situation for women. We can and do appropriate men's clothing at will. A woman dressed in a man's suit is considered stylish, and because she is, she never has to question her motives in wanting to wear it.

How to Handle the Situation

- Get counseling.
- Don't be judgmental.
- Don't confide in mutual friends.
- If you are disgusted and appalled, you have a right to say so— but keep the conversational focus on your feelings, not how "sick," "immoral," or whatever you think he is.

24 The Final Chapter

••

"I have been impotent on two occasions, with two different women. They both approached the problem in the same way: suck, suck, suck. They sucked to no avail. I was in a fury at myself, finally getting all the cocksucking I'd ever wanted and look what I was doing, wasting it. This was very stressful for me. I finally had to just stop thinking about it."

—A thirty-four-year-old management consultant

By the time he is forty, nearly every man has experienced an episode of impotence, the failure to achieve or sustain an erection during intercourse. The causes range from the physical—drugs, alcohol, medication, exhaustion—to the emotional—stress, anxiety, indifference to, or from, a partner. Impotence is, for most men, an infrequent occurrence. But its impact on the male psyche is often great.

A man fears nothing more than sexual failure, and being sexually humiliated by his failure in front of a woman. He still defines sex as intercourse, which is dependent on an erect penis. His inability to achieve erection constitutes failure for him, though his partner may have enjoyed the experience and had multiple orgasms via oral and manual stimulation.

Of the men I surveyed, nearly half had been impotent on at least one occasion. Of that group, only a third reported sanguine reactions to the experience. One man said, "I apologized and went to sleep, knowing I'd be fine the next day; and I was." But others said:

"I understand this happens occasionally, and I have tried to make it up to my partner with more touching, hugging, kissing, and oral sex. But nothing truly replaces cock."

"I sought medical advice. The doctor said there was nothing wrong with me."

"I didn't handle it well. My wife was fine with it."

"I used my tongue to eat her out. I spread her ass cheeks and ate her asshole. I did everything I could."

"I handled it very calmly by going to sleep. However, it's only happened once."

For many men, the first "failure" of the penis is the harbinger of old age, flagging sexual stamina, and death. They ask:

What is a woman really thinking about you when you can't get it up?

"*This has happened to me on a few occasions now with women I didn't know well. They have been understanding, kind, and sexually attentive to a fault. I wonder what they're really thinking as they labor over my flaccid member. Do they think I'm getting old?*" writes a forty-two-year-old St. Louisan.

When a man experiences impotence, he does not agonize over the sexual pleasure he is missing. What concerns him is his partner. Is he letting her down? Does she think badly of him? And no matter what else he does to please her, does she feel sex "didn't happen" because they didn't have intercourse?

"Sex is when the man gets it up," says a thirty-eight-year-old. "She has to feel like it's all foreplay if a man doesn't get it up."

And from another: "I was impotent twice, and both times she cried. She thought it was her fault, that I didn't want her anymore. So there's the added pressure of knowing she'll blame herself if I don't pull it off."

Again, women are responsible, too, for creating the narrow definition of sex: intercourse. By taking an occasional lapse of the penis as a personal indictment of our sexual attractiveness, we endorse the belief that any man should be able to have sex with an attractive woman anytime. While we expect them to understand that sometimes we can enjoy sex without orgasm, we don't grant them equal consideration. Sometimes they can enjoy holding, caressing, and pleasing us.

"I've had a few bouts of impotence," writes a husband of twenty-three years. "They wouldn't have worried me much—I understood the cause was extreme stress—if my wife hadn't taken it so badly.

She was talking about plastic surgery, for herself, because she was sure her face and figure, which are still quite lovely, were turning me off."

Prolonged or recurring impotence *can* indicate a problem with a relationship. Men still misread it, blaming themselves, not the relationship, for their inability to perform.

"Six months before I finally left my wife, I became impotent with her," says a forty-five-year-old attorney. "We both knew the marriage wasn't working, but we had made the decision in our heads to stay together. Unfortunately, my body wasn't going along with the decision. All the resentment and anger were sitting on the end of my prick. If my penis hadn't stopped functioning, we'd still be together, I suppose. After I left her, I was okay, not great for a while, but okay with other women. It was a devastating experience. Now I can look back and understand it. Then I thought I was losing it for life."

If impotence is a regular and recurring problem, I advise men to see a medical doctor and, following a clean bill of health, a therapist who can help him talk about the feelings he may be bottling up inside. Men's bodies aren't machines and won't always do what they, and we, think they should do. Women may be even more guilty than men of applying a mechanical solution to "the problem." We approach a flaccid penis as if it were a recalcitrant player who could be coached back onto the field.

When women write to me about male impotence, they invariably ask:

What should I do to make him hard again?

"I like to date older men and sometimes they can't perform. I have tried everything, giving them head until my jaws hurt and masturbating them. I know how to hold a penis so I can stuff a fairly soft one inside me and squeeze hard on it with my vaginal muscles. Is there a trick, a special place you can touch on a man, which will get him hard without so much work?" writes a reader.

Men tell me women perform fellatio most ardently when they are impotent. Some men want a woman to respond this way. They report that it achieves the desired effect—erection—at least some of the time. The majority of men, however, want their partners to pay less, not more, attention to a penis suddenly gone soft.

"If a reasonable degree of oral and manual stimulation fails to have the desired effect, I wish she would stop," writes a thirty-five-year-old. "If she doesn't dwell on it and continues kissing and caressing other parts of my body, I can concentrate on making love, and sometimes my fantasies, and not on trying to get hard. If I forget about it, I usually do get hard."

And from another man: "I have had problems with maintaining an erection with new partners. I get so tense about performing well for them that I can't perform at all. Usually this is a disaster. Once a woman handled the situation by ignoring it. She masturbated for me. She had a tremendous orgasm that got me so excited, I was hard again and had no trouble making love to her. We are living together now."

The majority of men would be delighted with a woman capable of such sexual abandon. Nothing excites a man more than a woman's pleasure. The best response to impotence is to seek your own pleasure or allow him to give it to you. Relax and enjoy—and hold the psychoanalysis.

"If she can relax, then I can," says a forty-nine-year-old. "The worst thing is to be smothered with female sensitivity and understanding. If I can't get it up, I don't want to hear a woman tell me it's okay, especially if she's hovering over me. I feel like I'm on my sexual deathbed, and she's the nurse lying to me about my prospects for survival. I want her to relax and let me give her a good time."

And from this "early-middle-aged" man: "I don't want my partner to make any more of my failure to maintain an erection than I do of her failure to reach orgasm every time. Women are just as goal-oriented in sex as we are. Everybody needs to lighten up. Isn't sex supposed to be fun, not work?"

Yes, it is supposed to be fun—something we've forgotten in our quest for the perfect-every-time coupling.

How You Should Handle His Impotence

- Ignore it and focus on yourself sexually.
- If it is happening on a regular basis, get him to a urologist to eliminate a medical cause, then get him to talk—not about his flaccid penis, but about his feelings. Maybe you've both been avoiding a problem in the relationship, and his body is forcing you to deal with it. Perhaps you haven't been as sexually responsive as you once were either—but your lack of ardor is more easily camouflaged.

Conclusion: A Need Greater Than Her Own

••

"Women think men only care about their own sexual pleasure—and women are very wrong. Men would rather please women than please themselves. In the abstract, I'd rather please a woman than like her."

—A fifty-three-year-old New York lawyer

The desire to touch is a human need, as much male as female. But the need to please sexually is stronger in the male. If women only realized this, we would have more sexual confidence in ourselves. We would make love with greater abandon because we would finally understand he isn't thinking about our heavy thighs when he's in bed with us.

Much of a woman's identity is still tied up in being a sex object. We play to man's sexual nature, which is visually oriented and lust-not love-driven, in the way we present ourselves to the world. On the one hand, we rail against the sexual status quo by berating him for the failure to love us properly and haranguing him for his attraction to porn. On the other hand, we perpetuate that status quo by dressing to attract and using sex to gain love and security, emotional and financial—and by shoring up the macho code at its every stress point.

A male friend, who is also a marital therapist, once told me: "The women who are happiest in their sexuality are those who are most comfortable with being sex objects. I don't mean that as a put-down of women at all. You can be a highly accomplished, successful, independent woman in the world and still realize that sexually, your role is to attract as long as his is to perform. The sexiest women are rarely classic beauties. They radiate the aura of sexuality. They project 'I am the desired object,' and every man believes they are. In an ideal world, each sex would be equal parts object and performer, but we don't live in an ideal world."

Man's identity is linked to his sexual performance. He still expects to pay for sex, both financially and/or through subordinating a part of his nature to the female will. The measure of his manhood is taken in penile inches and the minutes of sustained performance. We say that is not so, yet act as though it were, both by our own behavior and in our expectations of him.

Each sex has its special fears as we age. We fear the loss of sexual attractiveness; he, the loss of sexual potency. In this, as in many ways, we are at odds—equal yet not the same. There is no point in kidding ourselves that we ever will be the same in this lifetime. We can't really change a man into someone who loves like a woman. Nor would we want him if we could.

We could be much happier with him the way he is if we would let go of some anger, fear, and misconceptions—especially the belief that men are only interested in their own pleasure. He would rather please us than himself—in fact, he would often rather please us than like or love us. His need to please leaves him vulnerable. We can devastate the strongest man, naked in our bed, with a few cold words. He isn't the armor-plated stud we each pretend he is.

It is only fitting that a man have the last word here. This one comes from a northeastern college professor:

"With the complexities and ambiguities of sexual dynamics in this age of feminist awareness, some women seem not to be tolerant or realistically sympathetic enough about ways in which male sexuality strongly relates to visual stimuli. Some women are very judgmental about certain magazines, for example. I believe firmly there are troubling issues of gender differences that must be addressed. Sexual politics is played on the job and in the world. But we can't address those issues in the bedroom. These are tough times for many of us, men as well as women. They have been made tougher by the wholesale castigating of the male sex. This has got to stop. We need each other."

RECOMMENDED READING LIST

On Female Sexuality:

Ultimate Pleasure: The Secrets of Easily Orgasmic Women, by Marc and Judith Meshorer (Signet, paper).

For Yourself: The Fulfillment of Female Sexuality, Lonnie Barbach (Anchor Books, paper).

On Male Sexuality:

The Intimate Male: Candid Discussions About Women, Sex, and Relationships, Linda Levine and Lonnie Barbach (Signet, paper).

Male Sexuality, Bernie Zilbergeld (Bantam, paper).

The Hite Report on Male Sexuality, Shere Hite (Ballantine, paper).

Male Sexual Awareness, Barry McCarthy (Carroll & Graf, paper).

QUESTIONNAIRE

··

I developed the following questionnaire because I was interested in seeing whether or not a randomly selected group of men would reinforce the conclusions I'd already reached about men and sex. The questionnaire was distributed through a nationwide network of friends and professional associates and in response to ads I placed in city magazines. The results did reinforce my conclusions about men and sex—but I make no scientific claims on its behalf.

My name is Susan Crain Bakos. I write frequently for *Cosmopolitan*, *Penthouse Forum*, and other magazines on sex and relationships. The answers to your questions will be included in a book on men and sex to be published by St. Martin's Press next year. If you require extra space for some answers, use the backs of the pages. You do not need to divulge your name or address and phone number—unless you would like to be interviewed at greater length by telephone.

Thank you for participating in my research!

DEMOGRAPHIC BACKGROUND

Circle Answer:

Marital Status: Single   Married   Divorced
Age: 19–29   30–39   40–49   50–59   60–69   70+
Education Completed: HS   Some college   B degree
M degree   PhD

Race: White   Black   Hispanic   Oriental   Other
Religious Training: Protestant   Catholic   Jewish   Other
Is your religious belief: Strong?   Average?   Nominal?
Nonexistent?
Personal Income: Under $10,000 $10–20,000 $20–30,000
$30–40,000 $40–50,000 $50–75,000   Over $75,000
Where do you reside?:   Northeast   Southeast   Northwest
Southwest   Midwest   South   Upper Midwest
What is the approximate size of the town or city in which you live?

What is your job title?

DEMOGRAPHICS

Marital Status

Single: 29%
Married: 31%
Divorced: 39.5%
Widowed: less than 1%

Age*

19–29:   24%
30–39:   25%
40–49:   40%
50–59:   10%
60–69:   less than
70 +   1%

*Average survey respondent slightly older than average *P.L.* or *Forum* reader

Education

High school: 10%
Some college: 25%
Bachelor's degree: 50%
Master's degree: 10%
Ph.D.: 5%

Race

White: 69%
Black: 19%
Asian: less than 1%
Hispanic: 12%
Other: less than 1%

Religious Training

Protestant: 37%
Catholic: 28%
Jewish: 34%
Other: 1%

Religious Belief

Strong: 5%
Average: 40%
Nominal: 50%
Nonexistent: 5%

Income

Under $10,000: 1%
10–20,000: 5%
20–30,000: 11%
30–40,000: 50%

40–50,000:   13%
50–75,000:   15%
Over 75,000:   5%

Place of Residence

Northeast: 39%
Southeast: 21%
Northwest: 9%
Southwest: 7%
Midwest: 12%
South: 10%
Upper Midwest: 2%

75% reside in cities.

*Average survey respondent slightly older than average *P.L.* or *Forum* reader

SEXUAL EXPERIENCE

When did you begin masturbating? __Average age: 14__
Do you recall parental admonitions regarding this or other sexual

practices? __Majority: yes__

At what age did you lose your virginity? __Average age: 17;__

__but 20% were over 20.__

Have you ever had a homosexual experience? __31%: majority in__

__childhood__

Approximately how many sex partners have you had? __1 to 5,000__

Have you had fewer partners in the past two years? __Majority:__

__no__

Do you attibute this to (Circle all which apply)?:   Fear of Disease
Monogamous Involvement   Declining Libido   Lack of Time
Age-Induced Performance Anxiety   Other:
Of those answering yes, 61% cited monogamous involvement and/
or lack of time as main factors. Only 32% cited fear of disease.

Arousal

Are you turned on by (Circle all which apply)?:   Dirty Talk
Sexy Lingerie   X-rated videos   Pornographic literature and books
Female masturbation   Violent pornographic material   Other:

__92% turned on by all or most—sexy lingerie #1__

Do you find yourself *more* dependent on these or other erotic stimuli:

As you age? __49%: yes   42%: no   9%: can't say__

As the relationship ages? __73%: yes__

Are you generally satisfied with the quality (hardness factor) of your

erections? __32%: no;   68%: yes__

If not, why not? _____

How long has this been a problem? _____
Do you believe a *real* man should always want sex with an attractive

woman? __80%: yes__

Do you believe that same real man should *always* be able to perform

with such a woman? __85%: yes__

Have you recently experienced a situation that you felt should have aroused you, but didn't? (Describe) _____

_____

_____

PERFORMANCE

How long do you think intercouse should last? ___Two minutes to___

___all night; majority: 20–30 minutes___

In your typical experience, does it? ___91%: no___
Does the woman (women) in your life consider foreplay something

you do for her? Does she reciprocate? ___54%: do for her;___

___46%: reciprocate___

Would you like more foreplay from her? ___50%: more;___

___35%: satisfied;   15%: don't need___

In what form? _____

Can you locate her clitoris? _____

Can you describe how she likes you to touch it? ___57%: no___

_____

Does she reach orgasm without direct clitoral stimulation? _____

___53%: yes___

If so, how? _____

If not, does she (or you) stimulate her clitoris during intercourse?

55%: no
_____

Does she tell you what she wants and needs sexually? _____

If so, does she do it in a positive or negative way? Explain. ____

Overwhelmingly positive
_____

Has a woman ever faked orgasm with you? __40%: yes;__

40%: not sure; 20%: never
_____

How did you know? _____

How did you feel about it? __90%: somewhat to very upset__

Did you tell her? _____

Is your partner(s) usually orgasmic? __15%: always;__

70%: usually; 15%: multiple
_____

If not, does she blame you? Or do you blame yourself? __Less__

than 10%: blame you; 80%: blame themselves
_____

Do you get enough: Cunnilingus? __No: 55%__ Fellatio? __No: 75%__

Anal sex? __No: 50%__ Variety in positions, etc.? __No: 40%__

If not, what do you wish you had more often? _____

_____

What constitutes "great sex" for you? _____

_____

_____

EMOTIONAL INVOLVEMENT

Does love make sex better for you? How? __65%: yes__

_____

Have you ever experienced obsessive love? Describe. _____
Have you ever had difficulty performing sexually following a break-

up? __24%: yes;   70%: no;   the rest didn't know or answer.__

Does jealousy make you more intensely passionate? __33%: yes;__

__50%: no__

Are you (or have been) in a committed relationship? __85%: yes__

Were you monogamous? __50%: no__

If not, did you tell her? __5%__ Or did she find out? __60%__

Why did you cheat? __Majority: variety__

_____

What other sexual secrets do you keep from her? __70%:__

__masturbation__

PRIVATE CONCERNS

Do you consider your penis size (Circle): Small __41%__
Average __38%__ Large __21%__

How important is penis size to you? __Somewhat to very: 75%__

How important do you think it is to women? ___Somewhat to

very: 60%___

Do you have homosexual fantasies? Violent fantasies? ___32%___

have homosexual fantasies, 31% violent fantasies.___

- Should women draw a line between love and sex?

- When are fantasies harmful—and when are they helpful?

- Is "sex addiction" truly a sickness?

Bakos answers these and other questions with prescriptive advice that any woman can use to enjoy fulfilling sex and lasting relationships. In the author's singularly personal style, and in the words of hundreds of women from around the US, *Sexual Pleasures* brings wisdom, comfort, and sound counsel to women, *from* women.

SEXUAL PLEASURES
What Women Really Want.
What Women Really Need

SUSAN CRAIN BAKOS

Self-Help Guides

from St. Martin's Paperbacks

HOW TO SAVE YOUR TROUBLED MARRIAGE
Cristy Lane and Dr. Laura Ann Stevens
_____ 91360-5 $3.50 U.S.   _____ 91361-3 $4.50 Can.

THE WAY UP FROM DOWN
Priscilla Slagle, M.D.
_____ 91106-8 $4.50 U.S.   _____ 91107-6 $5.50 Can.

IN SEARCH OF MYSELF AND OTHER CHILDREN
Eda Le Shan
_____ 91272-2 $3.50 U.S.   _____ 91273-0 $4.50 Can.

LOOK BEFORE YOU LOVE
Melissa Sands
_____ 90672-2 $3.95 U.S.   _____ 90673-0 $4.95 Can.

SELF-ESTEEM
Mathew McKay and Patrick Fanning
_____ 90443-6 $4.95 U.S.   _____ 90444-4 $5.95 Can.

Publishers Book and Audio Mailing Service
P.O. Box 120159, Staten Island, NY 10312-0004
Please send me the book(s) I have checked above. I am enclosing $ _____ (please add
$1.50 for the first book, and $.50 for each additional book to cover postage and handling.
Send check or money order only—no CODs) or charge my VISA, MASTERCARD or
AMERICAN EXPRESS card.

Card number _____

Expiration date _____ Signature _____

Name _____

Address _____

City _____ State/Zip _____
Please allow six weeks for delivery. Prices subject to change without notice. Payment in
U.S. funds only. New York residents add applicable sales tax.